ASSESSING THE ENABLING ENVIRONMENT FOR DISASTER AND PANDEMIC RISK FINANCING

A COUNTRY DIAGNOSTICS TOOL KIT

MARCH 2025

ASIAN DEVELOPMENT BANK

ADB

6 ADB Avenue, Mandaluyong City, 1550 Metro Manila, Philippines
Tel +63 2 632 4444; Fax +63 2 636 2444
www.adb.org

ISBN 978-92-9277-248-2 (print), 978-92-9277-249-9 (PDF), 978-92-9277-250-5 (ebook)
Publication Stock No. TIM250104-2
DOI: http://dx.doi.org/10.22617/TIM250104-2

Note: In this publication, "$" refers to United States dollars.

Cover design by Edith Creus.

Photos (*clockwise from top*): **Coronavirus disease pandemic**. Medical technicians test the equipment inside the Pandemic Sub-National Reference Laboratory at the Jose B. Lingad Memorial Hospital in San Fernando, Pampanga; **Typhoon Ketsana (Ondoy)**. A month's worth of rainfall in a single day washed away homes and flooded large areas, killing hundreds and stranding thousands in Metro Manila and nearby provinces; **Nepal earthquake**. The 2015 earthquake damaged many school buildings in the Sindhupalchowk district (photos by the Asian Development Bank).

Contents

Foreword

The coronavirus disease (COVID-19) pandemic made clear that disaster risk financing options must consider pandemics, which, like natural hazards, can cause widespread economic and social disruption. Including pandemics in disaster risk planning ensures timely financial support to mitigate impacts and enhance resilience. Indeed, epidemics and pandemics are one of the most severe forms of disaster, with far-reaching impacts on public health, economies, and societies. Unlike disasters such as earthquakes and floods, which tend to affect specific regions, epidemics and pandemics are larger in scale and affect nearly all sectors of human life. For instance, the COVID-19 pandemic,[1] which some described as among humanity's worst crises since World War II, demonstrated the devastating effects on global health systems, economic structures, and social interactions.

The different characteristics of the impact of a severe epidemic or pandemic, when compared to disasters treated in the first version of the tool kit, have prompted the Asian Development Bank to publish this second version including the effects of both.

This second version of the tool kit—improving on the first version of this publication[2]—has, as its main addition, included an enabling environment for financial instruments that allow financing of measures to deal with pandemics and epidemics. The tool kit examines the critical importance of financing resilience to pandemics and severe epidemics as a disaster. It analyzes key areas for funding and the required enabling environment to develop and effectively use these tools in mitigating the impact on human lives and economic development.

The need for financing pandemics and epidemics is critical, as it ensures that governments and global institutions can respond effectively to these crises and minimize their devastating impacts. Financing is essential for strengthening health-care systems, supporting economic recovery, protecting vulnerable populations, and ensuring preparedness for future outbreaks. The COVID-19 pandemic has shown that the cost of inaction far outweighs the investments needed to prepare for and respond to pandemics. Therefore, the availability of effective financial instruments tailor-made to mitigate the impact of a severe epidemic or pandemic is critical.

1 H. Seddighi. 2020. COVID-19 as a Disaster: Focusing on Exposure and Vulnerability for Response. Disaster Medicine and Public Health Preparedness. 14 (4). e42–e43. https://doi.org/10.1017/dmp.2020.279.

2 Asian Development Bank (ADB). 2020. *Assessing the Enabling Environment for Disaster Risk Financing: A Country Diagnostics Tool kit*. https://www.adb.org/publications/disaster-risk-financing-country-diagnostics-tool kit.

Acknowledgments

This report was prepared under Strengthening the Enabling Environment for Disaster Risk Financing (Phase 1 and Phase 2), a technical assistance project executed by the Asian Development Bank (ADB).

Charlotte Benson (principal disaster risk management specialist, Climate Change and Disaster Risk Management Division, Sustainable Development and Climate Change Department, ADB) and Arup Chatterjee (principal financial sector specialist, Financial Sector Office, Sectors Group, ADB) provided direction and technical advice for the report.

The report was produced by a team of ADB consultants comprising Rodolfo Wehrhahn, team leader, insurance and capital market regulatory specialist (international consultant); Arman Oza, agriculture and microinsurance insurance specialist (international consultant); Roman Shynkarenko, agriculture insurance specialist (international consultant); Lawrence Savage, insurance regulation specialist (international consultant); Richard Walsh, public sector disaster risk specialist (international consultant); Mark O'Donnell, public finance specialist (international consultant); Hamid Rohilai, public finance specialist (international consultant); Nasreen Rashid, disaster insurance specialist (international consultant); Mayur Ankolekar, agricultural insurance specialist (international consultant); Thalia Alice Georgiou, health insurance specialist (international consultant); Christian Pfleiderer, health insurance specialist (international consultant); Gilbert Veisamasama, Jr. insurance industry specialist (national consultant); Udaya Raj Adhikari, insurance industry specialist (national consultant); Faraz Amjad, insurance industry specialist (national consultant); Kashmala Kakakhel, disaster risk financing specialist (national consultant); Ainsley Alles, insurance industry specialist (national consultant); Runsinarith Phim, insurance industry specialist (national consultant); Sheraz Khan, insurance/health industry specialist (national consultant); Shayne Rose Bulos, insurance industry specialist (national consultant); Bakhtyiar Bakasuulu, insurance industry specialist (national consultant); and Maria Cristina Pascual, project coordinator (national consultant).

The report benefited extensively from the generous participation of many government agencies, private sector organizations, and development partners in meetings and workshops organized under the project, including contributions to the very rich dialogue around the preparation of seven country case studies on the enabling environment for disaster risk financing in Cambodia, Fiji, the Kyrgyz Republic, Nepal, Pakistan, the Philippines, and Sri Lanka. The report team expresses great appreciation to the staff of these entities for their time and candid opinions.

Abbreviations

ADB	Asian Development Bank
COVID-19	coronavirus disease
DRF	disaster risk financing
DRM	disaster risk management
ILS	insurance-linked security
IRCM	insurance, reinsurance, and capital market

Executive Summary

Developing countries in Asia and the Pacific face considerable disaster risk, posing a significant threat to their sustainable development. Likewise, the severe economic impacts of medical costs and lockdowns of the coronavirus disease (COVID-19) pandemic have been long lasting. They reduced productivity, created unemployment, interrupted trade and supply chains, and have put testing capacity in many of the region's countries to finance the response to the calamity. This calls for measures to reduce disaster risk as well as pandemic or epidemic risk and to enhance management of residual or remaining risks. Indeed, recognition is growing of the importance of robust financial management arrangements in place for disasters triggered by natural hazards, epidemics, and pandemics. This can facilitate prompt and effective post-disaster response, limiting the economic and social consequences.

This report presents a comprehensive country diagnostics framework to help countries assess and strengthen financial management of disaster and pandemic or epidemic risk. It focuses on the enabling environment and ways to enhance it through greater availability and uptake of insurance and other risk transfer instruments.

The framework enables identification of the gaps between international good practice in disaster financing and the actual application in particular countries. It enhances understanding of demand and supply factors shaping the related enabling environment, including potential barriers to the more effective use of disaster financing instruments. It explores six critical axes shaping the development of disaster risk transfer instruments: government policy; economic conditions; product appeal; credibility of insurance, reinsurance, and capital market providers; Social protection policy; and unlicensed competition.

Application of the framework rests on a combination of desk work to gather background information on a country's disaster risk financing landscape and stakeholder questionnaires to confirm existing practices and provide insights into the barriers hindering the further development, uptake, and enhanced effectiveness of relevant disaster risk financing instruments.

The framework benefits from lessons derived from application of the framework to seven countries in Asia and the Pacific: Cambodia, Fiji, the Kyrgyz Republic, Nepal, Pakistan, the Philippines, and Sri Lanka. These country assessments identified various barriers and opportunities. Notwithstanding the diversity of the assessed countries, several common deficiencies hindering the enabling environment appear. Gaps that appear to be of central relevance when creating an enabling environment for disaster risk financing instruments are highlighted.

1

Introduction

1.1 Disaster and Pandemic Risk Financing: Objectives

Disasters delay long-term development and hamper efforts to reduce poverty in the developing member countries of the Asian Development Bank (ADB). Extreme weather and geophysical events set back development, directly damaging and destroying infrastructure and disrupting related economic activities and provision of services. In addition, the coronavirus disease (COVID-19) pandemic, had long-lasting and severe impact on economies over a large geographical area. The higher mortality and morbidity from the disease itself, severe impact on the economy in the form of medical costs, lockdowns that reduced productivity and created unemployment, and disruptions in trade and production have put to the test of the financial capacity of the country. These events place countries on lower long-term growth trajectories, push vulnerable communities deeper into poverty, and force adjustments in short- and longer-term development targets and goals. They can place significant fiscal strain on governments, businesses, and individual households, particularly if financial preparedness arrangements are limited. Delays and shortages in funding can significantly exacerbate the consequences of direct physical losses, slowing rebuilding and economic recovery, because of the indirect effects of a disaster, as shown by the COVID-19 pandemic.

Government officials, policy makers, and insurance regulators from ADB developing member countries across Asia and the Pacific have thus said they want to strengthen financial management of disaster and pandemic risk. They seek to smooth the cost of disasters over time and ensure timely availability of post-disaster and pandemic funding.

A strong enabling environment for disaster risk financing (DRF) is a priority prerequisite for achieving this objective. This includes creating a suitable environment for stimulation of risk transfer markets and making reliable reinsurance protection available. The effectiveness of disaster and pandemic risk transfer instruments demands well-developed and sound domestic insurance and capital markets. Government policy is also important, in that it can unintentionally crowd out the private insurance sector if not designed carefully. Likewise, cultural and religious dimensions are important.

The selection of specific DRF instruments needs to be adapted to the country context and disaster risk management (DRM) strategy. Established risk management theory provides countries with several options and associated financial instruments to manage disaster and pandemic risks:

- Risk avoidance: For instance, prohibiting the use of high-risk zones for construction and applying resilient building codes.
- Risk reduction: For instance, by retrofitting existing buildings.

- Risk transfer: Use of insurance, reinsurance, and capital market (IRCM) solutions.
- Risk retention or self-insurance: Use of own funds to finance the effects of a disaster.

The availability and suitability of specific sovereign DRF instruments partly depend on the economic conditions of a country. Large economies where the most severe disasters cause damage and losses equivalent to less than 1% of gross domestic product are able to retain their disaster risk on the country's own account. A country with available fiscal space can rely on post-disaster debt, raising much more easily than a country with a high ratio of debt-to-gross domestic product. Running a high budgetary deficit will diminish the ability of a country to find financial solutions post disaster.

A risk-layered approach helps identify the optimal bundle of DRF instruments: it breaks disaster risk down by frequency or probability of occurrence of hazard events and associated levels of loss for each layer of risk to identify the most cost-effective instruments for each layer (ADB 2014). Combining this information with other considerations, the speed with which disbursement is required, the relative cost-effectiveness of alternative instruments for specific layers of risk, and the size and structure of an economy, governments can select the most appropriate instruments for each layer of risk, based on a range of factors.

Risk retention instruments are typically most appropriate for more frequent, less damaging events. These include annual contingency budget allocations, disaster reserve funds, and contingent financing arrangements, all of which are put in place before disasters strike. After a disaster strikes, governments can also reallocate budgets, increase borrowing, and raise taxes to provide additional resources.

Market-based risk transfer solutions provide more cost-efficient financing for medium-level risks, generating higher levels of loss but less frequently. These are taken out in anticipation of disasters (including pandemics) and include insurance, reinsurance, and insurance-linked securities (such as catastrophe bonds). As indicated above, the effectiveness of those instruments depends on the availability of well-developed and sound IRCMs highly linked to the effectiveness of a conducive regulatory environment.

The diagnostic tool presented in this report assesses the impediments to the existence of an enabling environment for such DRF solutions that can effectively reduce the financial burden during and after a disaster, allowing for a faster recovery.

Financing disaster and pandemic risk is not only a government responsibility; the private sector and individuals should be encouraged and enabled to be financially prepared for potential disasters and pandemics. A similar risk-layering approach is applicable. Decisions on the reduction, retention, and transfer of disaster and pandemic risk should be made by households and businesses within the structure of a broader framework, selecting appropriate instruments for each layer of risk.

1.2 Pandemic and Severe Epidemic Risk Financing

Several reasons have motivated this second version to include pandemics and severe epidemics as hazards that need to be financed and require an enabling environment for those instruments to develop.

Public Health Impacts of Pandemics

Strain on the health-care systems. One of the most immediate and visible effects of a pandemic is the strain it places on the health-care systems. The demand for health-care services increases exponentially as more people fall ill, overwhelming hospitals and clinics, especially when dealing with contagious and deadly diseases. During the COVID-19 pandemic, many countries faced shortages of essential medical supplies such as ventilators, personal protective equipment, and hospital beds. This shortage highlighted the need for preemptive investments in health-care infrastructure, medical supply chains, and health-care worker support.

Moreover, pandemics can severely disrupt routine health-care services. Nonemergency procedures and regular health checkups may be postponed or canceled, which can lead to secondary health crises, such as untreated chronic diseases or delayed diagnosis of conditions like cancer. Financing is crucial for strengthening the health-care systems to ensure that they can maintain critical functions during pandemics. Investments in health-care infrastructure, human resources, and essential supplies can significantly affect a country's ability to respond effectively to a public health emergency.

Vaccine and treatment development. Financing is also essential for research and development of vaccines and treatments. Developing vaccines is a costly, time-consuming process that requires significant upfront funding. The rapid development of vaccines for COVID-19 was a result of unprecedented global collaboration and financial investment in research and development. Without this financial support, it would have taken much longer to develop effective vaccines, and the pandemic's toll could have been far worse. Continued financing in medical research is critical not only for the development of vaccines but also for creating antiviral treatments, diagnostic tools, and rapid testing technologies that can be deployed during future outbreaks.

Economic Impacts of Pandemics and Severe Epidemics

Loss of productivity and economic activity. Pandemics are not only a health crisis but also a major economic disaster. The restrictions imposed to curb the spread of disease—such as lockdowns, quarantines, and travel bans—can lead to significant disruptions in economic activity. Businesses close, supply chains are interrupted, and entire industries, such as tourism and hospitality, suffer severe losses. The International Monetary Fund estimated that the global economy contracted 3.5% in 2020 because of the COVID-19 pandemic, marking the worst peacetime recession since the Great Depression.

To mitigate these economic shocks, substantial financial support is needed to assist businesses, workers, and vulnerable populations. Governments need funds to provide economic stimulus packages, support small and medium-sized enterprises, and offer unemployment benefits to those who lose their jobs due to the pandemic. Financing such economic interventions is crucial to maintaining stability and preventing long-term economic damage that can persist well after the health crisis has subsided.

Social protection programs. Pandemics disproportionately affect vulnerable populations, including low-income families, informal sector workers, and those without access to social safety nets. Financial resources are needed to expand social protection programs, such as direct cash transfers, food assistance, and health-care subsidies. These programs help alleviate the economic hardships individuals and families face during pandemics. For instance, during the COVID-19 pandemic, many governments implemented emergency cash transfers and food distribution programs to prevent widespread poverty and hunger. Financing these programs ensures that the most vulnerable members of society can survive the crisis and recover without falling into extreme poverty.

Preparedness and Prevention

Investments in pandemic preparedness. A major lesson from the COVID-19 pandemic is the importance of being prepared for future outbreaks. Financing pandemic preparedness is one of the most cost-effective ways to mitigate the impact of pandemics. This includes investments in early warning systems, disease surveillance, and public health infrastructure. Early detection of outbreaks can help prevent local diseases from turning into global pandemics. For example, stronger surveillance systems could have identified the initial outbreak of COVID-19 earlier, potentially allowing for quicker containment and reducing the global spread of the virus.

Financing is also necessary for stockpiling essential medical supplies, such as personal protective equipment, ventilators, and medications, so that these resources are readily available in the event of a pandemic. Countries that were better prepared in terms of stockpiles and public health infrastructure were able to respond more effectively to COVID-19, underscoring the value of proactive financial investment in preparedness.

Strengthening global health institutions. In the case of pandemics, they are a global problem that requires a coordinated international response. Global health institutions, like the World Health Organization, play a crucial role in coordinating international efforts to control pandemics. Still, they need adequate financial support to carry out their missions. Financing global health initiatives ensures that all countries, particularly low- and middle-income nations, have the resources they need to prevent, detect, and respond to pandemics. Strengthening the capacity of international organizations to lead coordinated efforts in areas such as vaccine distribution, research, and information sharing is critical for effective pandemic response and control.

1.3 The Country Diagnostics Framework

The report presents a comprehensive country diagnostics framework that can be applied to support countries to assess and strengthen their financial management of disaster risk.[1] The tool allows governments to assess their level of financial protection against disasters and pandemics and to establish an overview of current policies and other demand and supply factors shaping their current level and forms of financial protection. It also focuses on the state of the enabling environment and opportunities for enhancement to support the increased availability and uptake of insurance and other risk transfer instruments. It serves as a foundation for identifying specific gaps, barriers, and challenges hindering the effective financial management of disaster and pandemic risk. Its application leads to a series of recommendations for strengthening the enabling environment, potentially including policy and legislative reforms, as well as the identification of specific new DRF instruments suitable to the local market and disaster and pandemic risk landscape.

[1] The methodology and the diagnostic tool were developed under the ADB regional technical assistance for Strengthening the Enabling Environment for Disaster Risk Financing (Phase 1 and Phase 2).

The tool provides the basis for new or deepened DRF engagement by international partners as part of the broader DRM and/or public financial management dialogue. The findings of a country's diagnostics can feed directly into developing a national DRF strategy, setting out priorities to meet post-disaster and pandemic financing needs strategically and effectively.

Sovereign disaster risk retention instruments are identified in the country diagnostics assessments as part of the gap analysis. The assessment uses a tool included in Appendix 1, that is an enhancement of the questionnaire developed by ADB and the World Bank (2017) (as summarized in the box below). Appendix 3 includes the tool when only the sovereign financing of the response to pandemics or epidemics is assessed.

Box: Examining the Full Sovereign Disaster Risk Financing Landscape

The disaster risk financing diagnostic tool developed by the Asian Development Bank and the World Bank assesses levels of financial protection against disasters to identify opportunities for enhancement. It contains questions for finance ministries to extend and expand on country analyses performed under technical assistance projects. These allow a more complete picture of the state of sovereign disaster risk financing arrangements, including risk retention mechanisms.

The questions cover the following issues:

1. Assessment of fiscal shocks associated with disasters
   - (i) contingent liability of the government,
   - (ii) fiscal risk assessment of disaster shocks, and
   - (iii) public disclosure of disaster-related fiscal exposure.
2. Ex-ante disaster risk financing
   - (i) annual contingency budget,
   - (ii) dedicated budget lines for disaster risk reduction,
   - (iii) dedicated disaster reserve funds,
   - (iv) line agency funding,
   - (v) contingent financing arrangements,
   - (vi) insurance of public assets,
   - (vii) any other forms of sovereign insurance, and
   - (viii) risk transfer arrangements through capital markets.
3. Ex-post disaster risk financing
   - (i) post-disaster budget reallocations,
   - (ii) external assistance, and
   - (iii) other ex post mechanisms.

Source: ADB and World Bank. 2017. Assessing Financial Protection Against Disasters: A Guidance Note on Conducting a Disaster Risk Finance Diagnostic.

The framework assessment on disaster risk transfer instruments covers sovereign and nonsovereign instruments. Governments can play an essential role in ensuring an enabling environment for nonsovereign and sovereign insurance and, in the process, reduce the contingent liability falling on them when disaster or pandemic strike.

The diagnostic tool draws on a modified version of the W&W Development Framework, which was refined to provide a methodology for assessing the DRF landscape and its enabling environment.[2] The diagnostic tool was used in seven countries (Fiji, Nepal, and Sri Lanka for natural hazards only; Cambodia, the Kyrgyz Republic, Pakistan, and the Philippines for natural hazards and pandemics or epidemics) and refined drawing on that experience (ADB 2019a, 2019b, 2019c, 2019d).

The framework focuses on six axes of relevance for the development of disaster insurance and capital market solutions:

(i) ***Economic conditions and support functions for the well-functioning of IRCM.*** These include things such as disposable budget for insurance, level of indebtedness, data availability, specialized financial sector courts, adequately equipped health facilities, doctors, vaccines, epidemic and pandemic research institutes, risk managers, insurance, and relevant professionals (e.g., actuaries, adjustors, accountants).
(ii) ***Government policy on the development of risk transfer instruments.*** This includes introduction of mandatory insurance protection, risk-pooling structures, insurance-linked securities (ILS),[3] pertinent regulations, and creating a level playing field for IRCM activities.
(iii) ***Credibility of the private sector offering risk transfer solutions.*** This covers regulatory environment, solvency of risk carriers, reputation of insurance and capital markets, professionality of distribution channels, loss adjusters, brokers, and availability of infrastructure (e.g., stock exchanges, payment systems).
(iv) ***Disaster and epidemic or pandemic risk product attractiveness, availability, and affordability.*** These include products for governments, corporates, small and medium-sized enterprises, farmers, individual households, and low-income populations.
(v) ***Social protection policy.*** This should recognize that low-income populations should enjoy social protection and at least basic health protection or support in obtaining insurance coverage. At the same time, this should not crowd out insurance solutions for people that can afford the premiums, and should explore the degree to which social protection complements or might be crowding out market-based solutions.
(vi) ***Unlicensed competition.*** This should recognize that the resilience of insurance providers depends on an adequate oversight. Unlicensed or entities poorly supervised by agencies with insufficient insurance supervision and risk management expertise can destroy the image of insurance and leave consumers without protection should a disaster cause their insolvency.

[2] The W&W Development Framework has been used on several occasions by Rodolfo Wehrhahn, a member of the consultant team for this report, to determine barriers to an enabling environment in work done for ADB, the International Monetary Fund, and the World Bank. The relevant axes for an enabling environment as determined in this framework follow Wehrhahn (2010).

[3] ILS bonds, including catastrophe bonds and other risk-linked securitization, represent assets whose value is largely driven by the occurrence of events not correlated to the financial markets, allowing for a high degree of diversification. With an ILS bond, the investor is exposed to a well-defined catastrophic or insurable event in addition to the credit risk of the issuer. For this additional exposure, investors are compensated with higher coupons; but, if no covered event occurs during the risk period, the bonds are redeemed at 100% of face value. When a covered event meets the thresholds in the risk transfer contract, investors stand to lose coupon payments and/or a percentage of the principal. The redemption price of the bonds is reduced accordingly. For more details, see Appendix 5.

1.4 Application of the Country Diagnostics Framework

The tool is applied through a combination of desk work, stakeholder questionnaires, interviews, and group discussions. This wide-ranging approach is taken to accommodate the international good practice of countries with successful results and to incorporate expert judgment on the actions needed to better enable the effective use of DRF instruments.

The basic steps are as follows:

- The first step is to gather background information on the country's DRM and DRF strategy and on the DRF instruments in use. This information is drawn from extensive publications, government websites, insurance and reinsurance industry documents, capital markets, and other analyses. Information is then also collected on the specific nature and magnitude of risk, covering all major natural hazards experienced by a country. Related gaps are also documented.
- The background information is then complemented with extensive questionnaires with open questions on areas relevant to the DRF approach and instruments used in the country. These questionnaires, integral to the diagnostic tool, are sent to relevant stakeholders for their inputs. The insights gained are critical for a robust assessment, and, as such, questions to the stakeholders are explained carefully, stressing the importance of providing comprehensive and open answers. Note that stakeholders will not necessarily respond to all questions. Experience shows that the questionnaire will provide wide-ranging responses, including contradictory statements, and leave some questions unanswered.
- The assessors review and filter the gathered information to draw preliminary conclusions. These conclusions are then verified with stakeholders repeatedly during the next steps.
- On-site interviews take place with selected stakeholders from both the public sector (the relevant ministries) and IRCM stakeholders, including actuaries, rating agencies, brokers, and auditing firms. These interviews enhance and complete the information gathered through the desk analysis and the questionnaire responses.
- The comprehensive information, after being filtered and confirmed, is then analyzed again, and gaps between international good practices and current practices are identified and confirmed.
- The recommended actions are discussed with stakeholders, and the feasibility and relevance confirmed before the country diagnostic is finalized.
- Implementation of the recommendations should be encouraged and followed.

2

The Six Axes of the Enabling Environment

This section examines optimal conditions shaping the enabling environment for insurance, reinsurance, and capital market (IRCM) instruments to take on disaster and pandemic or epidemic risk under each of the six axes. The corresponding series of questions for use in determining actual conditions against each axis are provided in Appendix 2. Appendix 4 contains questions for assessment only of pandemic or epidemic risk.

Appendix 5 describes in detail the most common IRCM tools used internationally, indicating the main uses, advantages, disadvantages, and preconditions for effectiveness in each case. Appendix 6 contains a glossary of key technical terms.

2.1 Government Policy

Comprehensive disaster and pandemic risk management policies and their effective implementation. Comprehensive disaster risk management (DRM) policies, programs, and guidance covering structural and nonstructural measures are critical in setting the foundation for sustainable and affordable IRCM instruments. For example, government engagement in comprehensive disaster and pandemic risk mapping and modeling—a public good requiring public involvement—and the dissemination of resulting risk information provide robust disaster and pandemic risk data critical to the design, including fair pricing, of IRCM solutions and an effective disaster risk financing (DRF) strategy. The propagation and effective enforcement of risk-sensitive building codes in full alignment with the natural hazards facing a particular country can considerably reduce the damage caused by disasters to homes. In turn, it will lead to a reduction in insurance premiums and a reduction of a government's contingent liability, including liabilities associated with damage and losses sustained by uninsured households. Similarly, risk reduction actions more generally by governments, the private sector, and individual households reduce future damage and loss and associated contingent liability. The availability of comprehensive universal health protection will allow the insurers to focus on the gaps in the available protection.

Comprehensive disaster and pandemic risk financing strategy. A comprehensive national DRF strategy provides an overview of the direction for enhancing the financial management of disaster risk based on a risk-layered approach. It includes clear articulation of the role of IRCM and other DRF solutions and of measures required to enhance the related enabling environment. It identifies the financial roles and responsibilities of different levels or domains of government and actions to enhance a country's financial arrangements for potential disasters and pandemic events. It also indicates the expected financial responsibilities of private corporations, small businesses, farmers, and households (differentiated by income group) in meeting their own recovery and reconstruction costs, thereby managing expectations about post-disaster and pandemic public support.

Effective IRCM policy formulation and execution. Clear policy statements advocating the use of IRCM solutions to strengthen financial resilience against disasters serve as a strong signal to market players to develop and promote relevant IRCM products. Financial authorities should give due attention to advance planning and preparation and, where appropriate, encourage the introduction or expansion of IRCM products, maintenance of effective and resilient payment systems, and sharing of knowledge and good practices on financial strategies (OECD 2013).

Well-coordinated disaster and pandemic risk management arrangements across all levels and domains of government. The ideal enabling environment will include clear articulation of DRM responsibilities and well-coordinated institutional arrangements across all levels and domains of government, from national and/or federal to local government, including transparent, rule-based systems for budgeting and allocation of related conditional and unconditional grants. Funds should be allocated appropriately to ensure effective disaster risk reduction and preparedness (including financial preparedness), and response actions can be undertaken at all levels of government. In addition, arrangements should be established to ensure prompt and effective disbursement of post-disaster and pandemic financing, including payouts from IRCM instruments, to spending units. The administrative framework for subnational government service delivery and expenditure responsibilities should also involve transparency, accountability, and performance measurement.

Well-complemented roles of national and/or federal and local governments regarding IRCM policy declaration and execution. Carefully aligned roles of national and/or federal and subnational governments facilitate competition, driving down IRCM prices.

An equitable legal framework for banking and insurance. Robust regulation and supervision, including requirements on capital adequacy and solvency in the event of institutional failure, as well as market conduct regulations against mis-selling by intermediaries, should be combined with effective use of information technology that facilitates the provision of transparent, efficient, and effective banking and insurance services. The availability of insurance services includes the provision of property, casualty, life, and health insurance protection to individuals and businesses based on risk-based premiums that reflect the actual cost of the loss exposure. Additional markups are factored in for transaction, administration, and capital and reinsurance costs. These markups are often high because the necessary data are not available, risk assessments are insufficient, and relevant investments are lacking due to underdeveloped capital markets. Effective liability laws should allow third-party reparation for loss and damage due to incomplete or inappropriate provision of goods or services, and they should be enforceable in a court of law if the provider seeks to avoid liability.

Customized regulation of IRCM solutions. Customized enabling regulations for the development, distribution, risk-based pricing, and implementation of DRF products encourage uptake and incentivize disaster risk reduction. Insurance might not always be the best solution to address disaster risks for poor people and may need to rely on premium support. Governments should subsidize disaster insurance products that are based on needs, adjusted to the local context, and embedded into holistic risk management and resilience-building strategies. The exercise of powers to remove difficulties, if any, in the timely procurement of IRCM solutions and post-disaster release of funds can go a long way in supporting the uptake of IRCM mechanisms.

Effective financial literacy programs. Governments can facilitate or provide high-level financial literacy programs in schools, universities, and technical or vocational education training colleges, strengthening the understanding of credit and debt management, risk management, and savings and budgeting strategies. They also encourage the effective use of appropriate insurance and investment products. IRCM consumer education should be included as part of national DRF strategies, with the active involvement of all stakeholders to ensure that programs are sustainable.

Tax incentives for the use of IRCM solutions. Well-designed business and personal tax incentives for the purchase of disaster IRCM solutions offer a much-needed impetus to sustainable market development without inflicting significant revenue losses on the government treasury.

Tax incentives for providers of IRCM solutions. Direct and indirect tax incentives to providers of IRCM offer a positive nudge to the market to develop suitable products and simultaneously help bridge the viability gap, if any, in distributing such products.

Tax-free premiums. Exemption of indirect taxes, such as value-added tax or general sales tax, on the premium payable on DRF products, can increase the demand for such products.

Premium subsidies for low-income and vulnerable groups. Full or partial premium subsidies on DRF products for the most vulnerable and poor sections of society provide a form of social protection. Premium subsidies, as opposed to ex-post-disaster and pandemic relief, also promote better government fiscal planning and effective budget management of public finances.

Financial aid for commercially uninsurable risks. Financial aid in the form of social protection, claims subsidies, or operational cost subsidies in respect of risks that are commercially uninsurable or unviable can fill the gap left because of market failures.

Mandatory primary health-care coverage for the population. This will help to reduce the risk of a pandemic or epidemic severity and outbreak.

Sustainable social health program. This program should regularly undergo an actuary evaluation.

Coverage for pandemics and epidemics under government-provided health-care schemes and/or social health insurance. This needs sufficient funding and infrastructure to provide the coverage.

Effective border control policies on health hazards. Border health teams should be included to screen for signs of communicable disease.

Strict policies governing animal–human interactions. These include, but not limited to, wet markets and wildlife trade with a strong regulator in place that takes enforcement action and has a track record of prosecutions.

Policies and procedures in place for pandemic and epidemic emergency preparedness. These include plans to limit contagion risks, plans for health-care infrastructure use, and stockpiling.

Robust policies for public health, particularly communicable disease control. Having robust and well-coordinated public health messaging results in a high level of population health literacy, particularly concerning hygiene, sanitation, and the management of communicable diseases.

2.2 Economic Conditions and Other Support Functions

An expanding economy and low inflation. An expanding economy with low inflation and a strong emphasis on corporate risk management, including business continuity, would generate higher written annual premiums with a higher number of exposures. The management of monetary policy by an independent central bank focused on low interest rates and modest growth in consumer prices can help increase the uptake of insurance in a modest manner with a small element of profit, provided there are no underwriting losses. A persistent low-interest rate environment has been a significant driver in attracting noninsurance industry capital into the insurance-linked security (ILS) and catastrophe bond markets.

Access to financial services. Expansion of trade and economic development, coupled with a growing emphasis on inclusive growth by governments, can result in higher levels of access to a wider range of affordable financial products and reliable services (savings, credit, insurance, and remittances) through more efficient intermediary channels and new technology. It also enables individuals to start and expand businesses, invest in education, manage risks better, and absorb financial shocks (Patwardhan 2018). Disaster insurance is considered to complement a package of resilience-building policies consisting of financial inclusion, access to health and nonhealth insurance, and stronger social protection shields, among others (McConaghy 2017). Moving forward, the movement along this trajectory should lead to a more diversified, dynamic, competitive, and resilient financial system.

Well-developed insurance and capital markets. Well-developed insurance and capital markets support the provision of a full suite of innovative and sustainable IRCM products. In alignment with a country's disaster risk landscape, these can accelerate early recovery and reconstruction by providing rapid post-disaster liquidity soon after the occurrence of an event. Insurance and capital markets nowadays are increasingly connected, and the links between them are deepening, as efficient capital seeks access to risk-related returns. Insurance markets offer opportunities for the transfer of disaster risks. Due to their peculiar loss distribution—with low payouts in most years but sudden spikes in disaster years—a large portion of such risks ends up with reinsurers (Hofman 2007).

Consequently, the probability of insurers depleting the capital in insurance markets because of large deviations from expected losses is significantly reduced. Rating agencies and regulators, therefore, give credit for reinsurance when calculating capital requirements for solvency purposes. However, reinsurance premiums remain highly volatile because reinsurers need to reflect the peaks in insurance losses in their price and also because international capacity is reduced. Increasingly, capital markets are providing risk capital that can be tapped through the use of ILS, such as catastrophe bonds. ILS efficiently allocates risks and potential losses over a large pool of investors, offering promising prospects of reducing the premium volatility associated with traditional reinsurance (Hofman 2007). Market participants should have the depth of management, credibility, and financial resources to implement new DRF approaches that incentivize disaster risk reduction before potential events and rebuild better in their aftermath. For example, insured businesses should be required to regularly check the metal-edge flashing, secure the roof cover to the edge of the building to reduce the risk of wind damage, and take appropriate measures to reduce flood risk.

Comprehensive disaster risk data. Data on hazards, exposure, vulnerability, and losses enhance the accuracy of risk assessment, contributing to more effective disaster risk management measures, including disaster risk financing instruments (OECD 2012). Probabilistic risk models indicate the likely order of magnitude of risk (UNISDR 2015). In the insurance sector, the quantification of disaster risks facilitates effective underwriting by setting risk-based premiums and managing disaster accumulation, given the strong correlation of disaster exposure with solvency capital. It is also important in building demand, particularly where insurers charge high uncertainty markups in the absence of such information. Such data are also useful for creating and modifying building codes by quantifying the potential risk during the lifetime of a building, bridge, or critical infrastructure facility. Having data also enables robust analysis of flood risks and drives investment in flood protection and the design of tailor-made insurance covers. A better understanding of hazard events can inform decisions on preparedness, location of critical facilities, and evacuation procedures. Critical health data will also allow the implementation of preventive measures and mitigating actions, in case of the outburst of severe epidemics or pandemics.

Readily accessible meteorological, weather forecasts and geophysical data. Ready and timely access to data from national or international agency on weather and climate forecasts provides accurate history of parameters such as precipitation levels, temperatures, tidal movements, wind speed, soil moisture levels, and seismic activity. By incorporating them into risk assessment models, public and private economic actors can directly assess how future weather or climate events might affect their financial loss or gain. These forecasts are critical for designing and operating alternative risk transfer products that provide protection against adverse effects of fluctuations in weather parameters. These solutions revolve around measurable indexes based on predefined parametric triggers or payout mechanisms (Marsh & McLennan Companies 2018). The main advantage over traditional indemnity-based insurance is that there is no lengthy claim procedure each time a loss happens. Additional investments in tamper-proof weather stations and river and earthquake monitoring equipment may be required to boost the availability of data.

Professional financial services. Financial advisory services, including accounting, actuarial services, auditing, public finance, information technology, risk modelers, and rating agencies, are building blocks for developing insurance and capital markets. By providing quantitative financial and economic information and risk analysis reports based on advanced technical tools, they help strengthen the financial management of disaster risks. Actuaries are widely employed in risk management, pricing, and reserving insurance products. They are also closely involved with the ongoing monitoring of the overall solvency of insurers, supporting the asset and liability matching process, and ensuring the adequacy of an insurer's reinsurance programs. Public finance experts help assess disaster-related contingent liabilities within public finance frameworks due to economic disruption in the aftermath of a disaster that can create significant budget volatility. Based on the assessments, they can recommend how to effectively manage these contingent liabilities and reduce the ultimate cost to governments of disaster-related events, thus helping build confidence in the soundness of public finances and the government's ability to respond to disasters (OECD 2018). Independent rating agencies will provide information to the public on the financial ratings of insurance companies and describe their financial strength succinctly after considering a wide range of factors, including the macroeconomic environment, risk-based capital adequacy, risk assessments, loss reserves, ceded insurance leverage, risk of an insurer's investments, and their ability to pay claims, especially in times of financial strain, for example, following major disasters. Auditors enhance the credibility of the insurance and capital market players by independently examining books of accounts to establish their accuracy. During this process, accountants, auditors, and actuaries should be licensed and regulated by their own professional bodies. They should be required to undergo continuing professional development, be committed to ethical and professional practice and standards, and be subject to a dispute resolution framework to benefit any dissatisfied clientele. Technological advances and higher-resolution exposure data enable risk modelers to conduct accurate risk assessments and quantify the financial impact of a range of potential future disasters. This information is vital for insurers to increase their understanding of disasters and to offer better protection solutions while remaining solvent.

Strong government technical disaster and pandemic risk management capacity. National governments must play a pivotal role in DRM by establishing institutions and disaster and pandemic risk governance, including mainstreaming DRM into development plans and policies. Resources need to be made available to ensure the completion of effective, across-the-board post-disaster forensic analysis by developing early warning systems to address forecasting needs, installing communications portals to address the needs of vulnerable groups, identifying areas for improvement and increased risks that may need to be identified post-disaster, promoting risk awareness, building fiscal resilience, and enabling access to disaster risk finance and insurance tools. Such analysis will help governments confidently predict where they might lead through strategy or policy actions. Government capacity is also required to implement disaster and pandemic risk reduction and disaster and pandemic risk response plans in partnership with the community, the private sector, potential donors, and nongovernment organizations. The insurance supervisory system, which constitutes an important aspect of a government's contribution to effective disaster resilience, should be included when considering its close links with the insurance sector, whose specific skills, capabilities, and experience include mapping, modeling, calibrating, pricing, and underwriting disaster risks with bespoke solutions. In addition, a wide range of laws and regulations related to ILS treatment, recognition of new technology in underwriting and claims servicing, taxation, procurement, and contracts, among others, are needed to facilitate the deployment of the insurance sector capacity.

A well-staffed and trained medical sector. High clinical training levels, particularly in disease detection, enable outbreaks to be effectively diagnosed and reported. Containment facilities in hospitals or other suitable locations are designed explicitly for infectious patients and disease outbreaks. Doctors, nurses, and hospital beds to population ratio is near the Organisation for Economic Co-operation and Development (OECD) average. Critical equipment (CT and MRI scanners, ventilators, personal protective equipment) are sufficient to cope with existing demand and surge demand during a pandemic. Cold storage capacity across countries is needed to cope with routine and surge demand (e.g., mass vaccination during a pandemic).

2.3 Product Availability and Affordability

Appropriate disaster insurance products. The range of risk transfer products available in a particular market should reflect a country's disaster risk landscape and social and economic context, with providers receptive to development of new types of products and risk transfer solutions. Traditional indemnity property insurance products have typically been designed in developed countries where the impact of major disaster events is significantly less damaging relative to economic size than is typical for emerging economies. Parametric insurance can be particularly useful when traditional markets lack the capacity or appetite, especially where risks are typically underinsured or uninsured or where the impact of an event is related to business interruption losses greater than the direct costs of the damage to physical assets (Marsh & McLennan Companies 2018). Solutions can also be tailored to reflect specific geography, risk exposure, risk appetite, and budgets (Willis Towers Watson 2017). They can cover both specific disaster losses and frequency losses—for example, business interruptions caused by a hurricane or the impacts of decreased precipitation (Marsh & McLennan Companies 2018). Access to robust independent data is critical for scaling up parametric solutions, as this addresses any moral hazard that may arise because of internal insurance company-controlled data. Potential for basis risk also exists because of differences between the actual payment received from the parametric product and the actual loss suffered. No insurance payout is made until the set trigger point is reached. Basis risk can be limited by blending parametric with more traditional insurance capacity to speed up recovery (Willis Towers Watson 2017). It is essential to consider how combining traditional indemnity policies and parametric solutions can work together to achieve the best results (Marsh & McLennan Companies 2018).

Consumer-friendly products and services. Ordinary financial consumers require access to insurance products that meet customer-friendly criteria to ensure transfer of substantial amounts of risk to the insurance sector and continuing confidence in the sector. These criteria include the following:

- jargon-free, unambiguous, and comprehensible policy wording in local languages clarifying limits of cover, the extent of exclusions, and the application of deductibles that will enable consumers to make informed choices based on common sense reading of the terms;
- avoidance of unnecessary coverage or services that increase costs;
- multiple channels of distribution, typically including both agents and/or brokers and remote digital modes, as well as mobile phone operators targeting specific customer needs;
- competitive insurance premium financing arrangements for spreading payments over an established period of time that allows for better control of cash flows and freeing up capital for other business-critical needs;
- prompt, fair, and equitable payment of claims in accordance with the provisions of the contract where the liability is reasonably clear;
- total confidentiality of policyholder information, unless it is legally necessary to disclose that information to statutory authorities (Chandwani 2020); and
- accounting for religious and cultural beliefs and ethnic customs, as applicable and appropriate, when designing insurance contracts and using distribution channels.

Strong consumer awareness. Prerequisites for the demand of disaster risk insurance products are strong consumer awareness and understanding of disaster risks, the level of preparedness, and the potential scale of losses; IRCM options available and their coverage; the ramifications of willful nondisclosure of material facts, underinsurance, high deductibles and the time of purchasing insurance, and the procedure for lodging a claim; as well as the features of disaster relief programs. One reason for low awareness about low-frequency risks is the lack of experience with such events. Tailor-made and continuous national customer awareness programs are often necessary to improve understanding of the risks, the role of insurance and other financing options, and the appropriate coverage for the most severe and widespread risks designed within a cost–benefit approach to encourage uptake. Such initiatives also help enhance credibility in the insurance and capital markets. The government should also ensure the insurance system includes a dispute resolution framework to deal with dissatisfied clientele on a cost-effective and equitable basis.

Business continuity cover, including pandemic and epidemic risks. Businesses may be unable to operate for a number of months following a disaster and pandemic as a direct consequence of physical damage to their properties, machinery, stocks, and other assets; as a consequence of damage to power, transport, and other infrastructure and services; and/or as a consequence of damage due to supply chain disruptions. Interruption of business income coverage compensates businesses, after a brief waiting period, for lost income resulting from property loss or damage until restoration is complete. In addition, the policy covers operating expenses, such as utilities, which continue even when the business has temporarily halted activity (Leavitt Group 2023). Contingent business interruption policies also reimburse businesses for expenses and lost profits cause by disruptions to the supply chain. During restoration following a loss, businesses may incur expenses to keep operating. Extra expense coverage reimburses businesses for reasonable excess costs over and above the normal operating expenses, including payroll to key employees, to avoid having to shut down during the restoration period (Leavitt Group 2023).

Mandatory market-based insurance for disaster risks. Risk-based mandatory disaster insurance can ensure that all those exposed to disaster risks are covered at least partially by insurance (Monti 2011). Correctly priced, affordable, and backed up with an effective enforcement mechanism linked to actionable measures by policyholders, such insurance encourages investment in cost-effective risk reduction measures and, as a consequence, helps reduce the social costs of disasters. Mandatory inclusion of disaster coverage in basic voluntary property insurance policies (e.g., fire, homeowners, motor) can be an effective vehicle for the widespread diffusion of insurance coverage (Monti 2011). Similarly, mandatory, loan-linked agricultural insurance offers a number of benefits. These include reduced marketing, distribution, and transaction costs; increased access to credit via reduced risk to lenders; increased risk awareness; and reduced adverse selection through wider participation. On the other hand, people typically underestimate substantial risks, such as the risk of major storm damage when living on a floodplain.

Mandatory international reinsurance or retrocession for disaster risks. Mandatory ceilings are imposed on domestic insurers on the level of insurance risk that can be transferred to international reinsurance markets. Such arrangements are useful when the insurance industry is not well developed. They enhance the possibility of diversification of risk but can also entail significant risks. If the cedent insurer does not have sufficient incentives to ensure quality underwriting, it can be viewed as a form of regulatory arbitrage where the reinsurer takes on significant risk in a jurisdiction without a primary insurance license. High retrocession limits could also impede the use of fronting arrangements where the cedent insurer leverages the underwriting or modeling expertise of the reinsurer and transfers a majority of the premium directly. Minimum retention requirements to discourage "fronting" or awarding preferences to domestic companies sometimes necessitate that a certain amount of risk be ceded to domestic (re)insurers to gradually build domestic retention capacity and reduce price volatility.

Uptake of capital market solutions. Solutions such as catastrophe bonds and other index-linked securities offer potentially cost-efficient mechanisms to transfer the risks associated with major disasters. These products require sophisticated issuers and buyers and may require regional participation. Pandemic bonds, such as those issued by the World Bank's Pandemic Emergency Financing Facility, provided financial support during crises like COVID-19 by transferring pandemic risks to investors. However, they faced criticism for delayed payouts and complex trigger conditions, which limited their effectiveness in providing timely aid. Although issuance activity from Asia and the Pacific has been limited in the past, the dynamics are changing, with cedent insurers and investors now having access to a broad range of collateralized structures to hedge and assume insurance risk. With Asian regulators putting regulations in place for special-purpose reinsurance vehicles, including protected cell companies for collateralized reinsurance, it will be natural for the ILS market in the region to grow.

2.4 Credibility of Insurance and Capital Market Stakeholders

Reputable regulator. A modern, well-resourced supervisory agency or regulator helps coordinate and catalyze efforts to put an enabling environment in place to transfer risks from governments, businesses, and households by ensuring that licensed insurers with adequate capital and sound governance and risk management largely conform with the Insurance Core Principles of the International Association of Insurance Supervisors and the Objectives and Principles of Securities Regulation of the International Organization of Securities Commissions. With observance of international standards and good practice, regulators can quell regulatory uncertainty and instill trust through sound regulatory frameworks; enhance understanding of the state of risk of the domestic and international market; and coordinate with government agencies, other regulators, and financial institutions. Sound institutions, robust regulatory framework, strict enforcement, and transparency in disclosure issues also have positive spin-offs while supporting resilience efforts. After a disaster, structured and well-governed payments can flow quickly from insurers to the locations of need and aid faster recovery. Insurance is also important in incentivizing preplanning by providing risk-based pricing incentives, besides serving as a vehicle through which (some) aspects of the resilience dividend can be monetized and, hence, used to provide stronger financial incentives for resilience. A reputable supervisory agency has the confidence of the public and the insurance industry and is well-positioned to promote and regulate innovative risk transfer solutions.

Reliable rating agencies. Reliable rating agencies increase insurance market efficiency by reducing information costs for agents and policyholders. These ratings are particularly important for insurers, providing assessments of their ability to meet claims obligations.

Reinsurers may need investment-grade ratings to retain consumers; brokers use ratings to place policies with higher-rated insurers (Feldblum 2011). Catastrophe bond ratings are based on a rating agency's assessment of loss probabilities and financial severity and generally have noninvestment-grade ratings because investors face a higher risk of losing their principal. The rating agencies rely, in part, on the risk assessments of major disaster risk modeling firms—the same firms that are used by traditional reinsurers to help them understand disaster risk.

Active public disclosure on insurance and capital market performance. Sharing relevant, comprehensive, and adequate information on a timely basis with the public in a nonrestricted and transparent manner provides a clear view of the business activities, performance, and financial positions of the insurance and capital market players. The disclosure of quantitative and qualitative information on their profile, governance and controls, financial position, and technical performance is expected to enhance the understanding of the risks to which the insurers and financial institutions are exposed and how they manage those risks (Starita and Malafronte 2014). When decision-makers are well informed on insurance and capital markets developments, they can make sound and effective DRF decisions that can improve conditions for increasing savings, taking up credits, promoting risk reduction behavior, and investing in more profitable and higher-risk activities. As policyholders, particularly poor people, tend to be unwilling or unable to pay for this, governments or other agencies have a role to play in ensuring this information reaches the most vulnerable, likely as a public good.

Solvent insurance and capital market players. Insurers limit their overall disaster risk exposure to an acceptable level out of concerns about solvency and the cost of capital. They accomplish this through (i) reinsurance, (ii) pricing insurance rates using "catastrophe loads" to account for potential disaster-related losses, and (iii) alternative risk transfer instruments that allow insurers to transfer fully collateralized liabilities through ILS to the global capital markets (Rawle 2013). By spreading disaster losses, there would be least disruption in insurance markets, particularly in terms of coverage restrictions, price escalations, and insurer pullouts. Financially strong, reputable, and efficient insurance carriers facilitate DRF growth by offering adequate capacity to withstand extreme events with minimal disruption. In many developing countries, insurers and reinsurers limit their disaster risk retention and are not interested in generating and exposing significant capital for underwriting disasters. This is because of general undercapitalization fears of significant claims arising from disasters that will lead to higher payouts, lower profitability, and reduced capital strength. While foreign insurers and reinsurers, with longer and broader expertise, remain willing to shoulder the significant risks via reinsurance, they essentially design and price the insurance products based on their global experience. Due to the absence of credible data and low retention, it is generally perceived that they have low incentives to monitor compliance with building codes or to promote risk reduction measures.

Consequently, reinsurers impose policy coverage restrictions, undermining a policyholder's ability to access insurance protection at a justified and reasonable cost. The transfer of risk to reinsurance markets can create counterparty, execution, and liquidity risks for cedents, which need to be effectively managed. Addressing these risks has been recognized in the Insurance Core Principles of the International Association of Insurance Supervisors. Supervisory or regulatory measures require or encourage local presence, the pledging of local assets, and/or local retention as a means of mitigating these risks.

High-quality insurance agents, insurance brokers, reinsurers, and reinsurance brokers. Market access to the in-depth expertise of insurance agents and insurance and reinsurance brokers is essential to successful business development and marketplace credibility, which, in turn, are a vital foundation for successful risk transfer markets. Reinsurers must have high levels of expertise and the capital needed to effectively take on risk, evaluate risk carriers, and design reinsurance programs that will transfer risk efficiently and effectively. Insurance and reinsurance are highly technical, complex businesses requiring significant capability in the fields of actuarial science and risk analysis.

Confidence and impeccable image of the insurance and capital market sectors. Strong public confidence in the insurance and capital markets makes it easier for governments to justify and enter into risk-sharing and transfer arrangements that rely on these sectors. Sound governance practices that promote fair, responsible, and professional dealings with the public and policyholders are key elements in fostering the public's trust and confidence. A negative perception in public opinion affects consumer attitudes and could seriously undermine the enabling efforts.

Fair pricing and claims-paying culture. The two primary functions of insurers are to provide adequate coverage at a reasonable premium rate and to pay losses promptly and fairly. Consumers are often unaware of the quality of an insurance product purchased and the extent of coverage. To reduce the risk of underinsurance, the product being offered must include a minimum level of coverage that is widely known. The premium rates should not be excessive, inadequate, or unfairly discriminatory. The premium being charged must be actuarially justified, and the use of nonrisk-based factors should not be allowed in the pricing, as this practice can restrict access to insurance in some areas. Besides pricing, customers entering into insurance contracts must have the confidence that provisions are in place to put into operation prompt, fair, and equitable settlements of claims in which liability has become reasonably clear (White 1998). Effective risk reduction, risk retention, and risk transfer all depend on the existence of a fair pricing culture.

Accessible and effective complaints and redress mechanisms. The presence of a sound internal and external complaint management framework helps insurers comply with regulatory requirements, gain insight into operational processes involved in complaint handling, and assess the levels of consumer satisfaction (Wolters Kluwer 2018). Common reasons that insurers deny claims include policy exclusions, failure to meet policy terms and conditions, nonrenewal of policy, failure to disclose a material risk, or failure to properly look after the property to reduce the risk of damage. If the insurance company and the customer disagree on the insurer's decision, they can take advantage of the internal complaints process within the insurance company and seek a review. If, after an internal review, they are still unhappy with the insurer's decision, they can use the external independent dispute resolution mechanisms, such as an ombudsperson. These types of complaint redress systems that ensure disputes between insurers and policyholders are resolved in a fair and straightforward fashion are a necessary component in the development and maintenance of industry credibility.

Transparent costs of insurance, reinsurance, and capital market solutions. Transparency is critically important as IRCM solutions can be relatively complex. Such solutions are able to rapidly pay out claims and provide much-needed liquidity soon after a disaster has struck.

They also provide transparency and assurance about the amount of money received in a payout and how and when it will be delivered. In some ways, they can provide a way for governments to commit to systems and rules for spending money and to take measures against fraud and misuse of public funds. Individuals designing and approving IRCM solutions must be able to have confidence that all material costs will be clearly laid out and accurately estimated. Accountability is critical in stalling a rollback in development gains and preventing vulnerable nonpoor people from slipping into poverty.

Understandable products. Effective oversight of IRCM products is fundamental to maintaining fair, safe, and stable insurance markets. Those who have to approve the products should be able to identify, mitigate, and adopt measures against risks to customers arising out of the products. A number of issues revolve around determining whether an insurance or reinsurance contract transfers significant insurance or reinsurance risk (Financial Accounting Standards Board 2008). This further helps in concluding whether a contract is defined as an insurance or reinsurance arrangement or as a financing arrangement (similar to a loan). In addition, certain contracts contain risk-limiting features that can complicate the risk transfer analysis. Against this backdrop, a proper understanding of insurance contracts and the bifurcation of risk transfer and financing segments is vital. Otherwise, it will make it difficult—if not impossible—to successfully justify the need for, and generally promote, the types of products involved.

No misleading advertising. Insurers and intermediaries should promote products and services in a manner that is clear, fair, and not misleading (Workman 2015). Disclosures should be easily understandable, provide information on key features of the product (approaches), and should not obscure important statements or warnings (e.g., exclusions). Clear and accurate advertising is important in building government and public confidence in proposed enabling solutions.

Guarantee fund for insolvencies of insurers and broker–dealers. When substantial amounts of risk are being transferred to and through insurers and broker–dealers, there are business risks involved. There may be an occasional failure of a primary insurer, especially in emerging markets, where consumer awareness of and confidence in financial markets are already fragile, so it might completely undermine public confidence in the adopted solutions. Therefore, if the environment can support a mechanism, such as a guarantee fund that takes over the claim payment responsibilities for an insolvent insurance company, it will be a desirable complement to the enabling environment. A guarantee fund is designed to protect smaller insureds. It typically has a cap on the amount payable per individual claim or a net worth exclusion, which excludes claims by companies whose net worth exceeds a statutory limit (Schiffer 2004). A reinsurer's obligation to make payments to the primary insurer does not diminish if the reinsured becomes insolvent and all payments under the reinsurance agreement are made to the liquidator. Policyholders cannot directly seek reinsurance proceeds because there is no contractual privity between the insured and the reinsurer. It may be noted that reinsurers are not backed by guarantee funds, and most property and casualty guarantee funds exclude coverage surety, financial guarantee, and assumed reinsurance. Clearing corporations require broker–dealers to maintain margin and make deposits to a general guarantee fund, which can be used to satisfy the outstanding obligation of any clearing member in the event of default to meet its obligations if its margin capital and own-guarantee fund deposits are insufficient to fully satisfy its debts.

2.5 Social Protection Policy

Effective social protection strategy. Social protection can help strengthen people's social and economic resilience against disasters. An effective and resilient system incorporates a number of pillars, including those from both the public and private sectors. Combining public social protection measures with private sector risk transfer mechanisms such as IRCM solutions provides a wide range of complementary solutions that meet the broadest possible range of disaster-related needs. Such an integrated approach is likely to be more efficient as well as effective. It will also help develop a stable market for the uptake of voluntary insurance by creating demand at the bottom of the pyramid.

Focus on nontransferable risks. Disaster risk financing strategies should incorporate social protection to support poor and vulnerable people suffering from the impacts of recurrent natural hazards resulting in failure of harvests, decline in employment opportunities, fall in real wages, and failure of informal safety nets resulting in a sequence of knock-on shocks to local economies and societies. In relation to these failures, social assistance does not provide the most balanced and cost-effective overall program. This includes safety nets, food subsidies, cash transfers, and weather insurance that overwhelms all other possibilities. Social protection instruments should be considered as part of a larger set of risk management arrangements, complementing and strengthening other mechanisms and systems. However, they should not crowd out other risk management arrangements (informal, market-based, or public) (Vathana et al. 2013) and render the market underserved. They also distort the market and deprive the market segment of innovative options that can be more comprehensive, cost-efficient, or effective. The private sector is geared up to efficiently and effectively cover risks, whereas this may not be the case for much of the public sector. Therefore, by utilizing private sector suppliers of social protection measures to the extent possible, global costs are likely to be kept to a minimum. Therefore, the private and public sectors need to attain a level playing field at the very beginning. Ideally, steps will be taken to ensure that public sector social protection will only fill gaps left by the private sector.

Existing analysis of risks that can be transferred to the private sector to increase effectiveness and budgetary costs. By providing data, methodologies, and tools for risk assessments, the private sector is a key actor in reducing losses, prioritizing risk-proofed investments, and the economic resilience of disaster-prone communities (UNISDR 2017a). This is the first step in determining how best to allocate social protection measures between the public and private sectors. If the analysis has been completed or is well underway, the enabling environment will be that much further ahead than would otherwise be the case. Social protection policies that clearly earmark risks and interventions to be carried out by the private and public sectors will ensure better utilization of financial resources and enable better fiscal planning by reducing cost uncertainties that typically surround social protection initiatives.

No crowding out of private sector initiatives. Regulators in countries moving from monopolistic and other restrictive regimes should strive to ensure that public sector domination over the markets does not crowd out private sector initiatives. In many jurisdictions, markets have been opened for private players after long spells of public sector monopoly. In such cases, a certain degree of caution needs to be exercised to ensure that "abusive practices do not undermine confidence in an embryonic competitive insurance market and consumers are sufficiently informed to protect their own interests" (Skipper and Klein 2000). Justifiable government intervention should be efficient and minimally intrusive. Regulatory forbearance may have to be given to private players. The continuation of a tariff allows insurers to follow a price that is set "so high that even the most inefficiently operated insurer is guaranteed a profit and, therefore, survival. Such an approach, however, results in high-priced insurance and excessive profits at the expense of consumers and businesses" (Skipper and Klein 2000). Alternatively, a de-tariffed regime allows price competition, bolstered by reasonable capital standards and close monitoring of insurers' solvency. This approach yields lower insurance prices, thus benefiting the consumer.

Cost equivalence for similar protection by the government and the private sector. The intent of public insurance plans is to use the administrative efficiencies of government-run schemes, as well as the purchasing power of the government, to control costs and rising expenditure on insurance. If costs between the two types of social protection suppliers are vastly different, the system will necessarily be skewed toward the lower-cost provider. However, the overuse of monopsony power may be inevitable because of budgeting constraints, potentially leading to reduced access, lower quality, and the explicit rationing of insurance. Government plans may also have unfair advantages over private plans as premiums may not be determined according to sound actuarial models but through controls. This hampers the longer-term sustainability of social protection programs as they do not need to maintain reserves, earn profits to attract capital, or pay premium taxes, in turn potentially crowding out of the private sector.

No carving out risks necessary for insurance, reinsurance, and capital market solutions to be sustainable. In commercial insurance, regulatory restrictions often impose underwriting restrictions on insurers and limit insurers' ability to charge different insurance premiums to consumers. There is a cross-subsidy in insurance premiums from low-risk consumers to high-risk consumers (Tennyson 2010). By avoiding carve-outs, the enabling environment is enhanced because insurance can function most effectively when the covered items include the widest possible selection of risks. In other words, cherry-picking risks for the private sector while ignoring the cross-subsidy element could prove to be counterproductive in terms of increased costs and/or loss of interest by the private sector in offering coverage. Therefore, allocating risks between the private and public sectors needs to be done while keeping in view the sustainability aspect for each of the sectors, as well as the need to ensure a continuous supply of a wide range of products and services to the target market segment.

Limited reconstruction loans after disaster events. To optimize the potential benefits of private sector insurance in combination with public sector support—that is, to be able to design the most efficient and effective global program—one does not want the public sector to crowd out the private sector. However, this would occur if unlimited reconstruction loans were available without embedding disaster insurance in the loan contract to consumers. Otherwise, ex-post facto welfare measures would tend to create disincentives for active risk management at the household level through the use of IRCM instruments. While ex-post facto welfare may become necessary in major disasters affecting uninsured populations, public policy must be carefully positioned between ex-ante and ex-post measures. This approach will clearly promote and incentivize the use of ex-ante solutions for cost-effective and timely relief to populations in times of disaster. It may also require public policy experts to convey a combination of appropriately targeted and phrased messages over a period.

Initiatives to promote microinsurance and Takaful insurance. These are important to the enabling environment because such initiatives can play an important role in wide-ranging

DRF solutions. If not available, the range of potential DRF system design possibilities will necessarily be constrained. Social protection through social insurance (subsidized microinsurance) carried by the private sector brings in the much-needed "entitlement" into the system, making it efficient. The classical government-funded social protection strategies through the welfare route often become trapped in bureaucratic shackles, thereby delaying benefit delivery in times of dire need. Regulated, private market insurance players can perform such functions more efficiently.

Shock-responsive social protection schemes are in place. Schemes should cover poor people and those who fall or are at risk of falling into poverty and/or informality because of disasters, including pandemic-induced economic downturns (schemes sufficiently financed, able to respond quickly, enabling database of beneficiaries, and efficient payout mechanisms in place).

2.6 Competition to the Formal Sector from Informal and Unlicensed Providers

Informal insurance providers play a critical role in insurance sector development, and large informal markets can be a key indicator of unmet formal market demand for insurance products and potential barriers to formalization and market development. They comprise a wide range of entities, from completely informal societies that are often of a community and mutual nature operating in the absence of regulation to formal legal entities (e.g., funeral parlors) that are exempted from insurance regulation. Competition from unlicensed players can be good or bad, depending on the circumstances. It can be disastrous if unregulated insurance schemes forgo any actuarial analysis. Such entities can be considered unsafe and unsound as they expose their members to further risks. Since informal sector vehicles operate in the shadow of formal financial institutions and are unregulated, they can be exploited to perpetrate fraud, which can badly damage the credibility of the local insurance market. On the other hand, an infinitely more desirable category of unlicensed players consists of reputable insurers licensed in other jurisdictions and able to provide products not otherwise available in the nascent local market, perhaps because of its small size, among other reasons. This type of unlicensed activity not only provides needed coverage but may also serve to stimulate players in the licensed market to fill these market gaps by means of more vigorous product development. In that way, the unlicensed companies raise the bar for the licensed market insurers, leading to new products becoming more widely available. However, the absence of a memorandum of understanding between the home regulator and the host regulator may actually present similar risks and challenges to the informal sector.

Strict criteria governing unlicensed competition. Needless to say, consumers have to be properly protected. To that end, there are usually three criteria for permitting unlicensed competition within a marketplace. First, there has to be some sort of control for market access by defining what constitutes an unlicensed insurance activity to ensure entities are properly capitalized and licensed within their home jurisdiction. Second, ways are needed to establish that products to be sold are genuinely not presently available in the local market. If this were not the case, licensed insurers would have no incentive to maintain their licensed status. Third, prospective policyholders must fully understand and accept that use of an unlicensed insurer means no access to protection under the local legal and/or supervisory system in the event of a claim. Experience shows under these strict criteria, reputable but unlicensed insurers participating in the local market can get more local residents to use risk transfer products and benefit development of new products and services by the licensed market players.

Regulatory enforcement of unlicensed providers. Formal sector regulators need to be privy to the activities of unlicensed players in their jurisdiction and be able to question them whenever required. Ideally, they should have a list of exempted insurers and impose a simple filing requirement to ascertain the risks they are covering and the scale of operations. There should be clarity about circumstances when they need to be licensed. Where disreputable entities are involved, regulators must have the power to act quickly to issue cease and desist orders that can be strongly enforced with the backing of the law. The regulatory framework must also provide the authority to quickly block the activities of any other unlicensed insurers who may have appeared to meet the criteria governing unlicensed competition but do not live up to their prior commitments.

Public awareness of the dangers of unlicensed providers. Awareness campaigns advising the public to be careful and sensible in choosing insurance providers and products can go a long way in preventing unlicensed and/or fraudulent players from penetrating the market. The general public, especially the low-income and less literate segments, are often easy prey for fraudulent schemes floated by fly-by-night operators. Such schemes and products offer attractive features such as spectacular returns on investment and other benefits to lure the meek investor or customer. The local supervisory agency website could have a list of all licensed brokers and insurers so that the public is able to differentiate licensed from unlicensed carriers. The site could also include the names of insurance companies authorized to fill particular market niches on an unlicensed basis.

Strong general insolvency law. A strong insolvency or bankruptcy law clearly specifying the rights of investors and creditors, as well as laying down a transparent and simple process for liquidation of assets, can help investors recover a portion of their money invested in fraudulent investment schemes or due to them when legitimate insurers have become insolvent. The insolvency law needs to include specific provisions with respect to insurance company insolvencies. If this is not done, the disposition of insurance-specific items such as unearned premiums will not be spelled out in the law, causing legal uncertainty and long delays in the ability to liquidate the estates of these types of companies.

Regulation of foreign players—both producers and distributors and/or intermediaries. Regulations need to be carefully designed to promote a level playing field and competition on equal terms between intermediaries (either tied or not tied to the insurance company) to ensure that, in all cases, the same level of consumer protection will apply. In almost every jurisdiction, financial markets today are a mix of domestic and foreign players. Insurance agents and brokers, reinsurance brokers, and loss adjusters operate in multiple jurisdictions, and a failure to implement a consistent approach across the industry to establish a level playing field for both domestic and foreign players could result in significant negative consumer and industry consequences. It would significantly reduce any regulatory arbitrage that could potentially undermine the good intention of protecting investors.

Antipredatory pricing regulations and technical pricing requirements. The pricing practices of insurers can create unfair outcomes for many consumers. The demand for almost all IRCM products is highly price elastic. As a result, price becomes a major area of competition among market players who engage in cutthroat tactics and try to "muscle in" by undercutting premium rates. At the same time, in the case of insurance, the price charged for a product has a direct bearing on the solvency of the provider and its ability to pay claims. If insurers take on too much business without a commensurate business plan and with insufficient income to cover their costs and claim expenses or inadequate capital and reserves to cover their liabilities, they can be driven into insolvency. Regulations, therefore, also need to ensure that undercutting premiums does not lead to marketwide solvency issues in the medium to long term. To achieve this, the market requires clear guidelines on technical risk-based pricing standards for new and existing products, as well as a provision that enables the regulator to step in wherever necessary.

Avoidance of private and public sector monopolies. Several countries have monopolistic markets, and many others are oligopolistic because of historical developments, economic trends, restrictive government control over entry and competition, or market practices (Skipper and Klein 2000). The regulator should strive for removal of government restrictions on entry and competition to ensure that monopolies or dominant market conditions do not emerge in their jurisdictions.

Regulation on retention of risks within the country. Subject to the availability of affordable products, most jurisdictions would prefer optimizing the retention of risks within a country that is subject to proper and adequate diversification of risks. The additional risk-bearing capacity need not be locally owned and locally established. Foreign-owned insurers can also bring additional capacity to the market, which can mean greater domestic retention. Also, it could be an incentive for insureds to bring their business, formerly located offshore, into the national market. Additional national insurance capacity serves the twin objectives of conservation of foreign exchange pertaining to reinsurance and enhancement of the profitability of domestic insurance companies by limiting the passing on of profit to reinsurers. While too little reinsurance can expose domestic insurers to excessive risk and exposure, ineffective reinsurance can also result in greater retention of losses, should they occur. Insurers sometimes enter into capital-gearing treaties to improve their solvency margin ratio, which are financial arrangements and not primarily a risk transfer mechanism. Therefore, greater risk retention should be balanced by requirements for higher levels of capital and the creation of appropriate reserves to protect consumers.

Nondiscriminatory tax treatment. Similar IRCM products should receive the same tax treatment regardless of provider. Discriminatory tax structures among various IRCM operators or among the same types of products offered by different providers can significantly affect their financial viability. Asymmetries in the tax code can lead to regulatory arbitrage, and this could pose dangers when it undermines the effectiveness of certain financial regulations. It can render the capital structure of a provider and the risks it faces more opaque. Distorting healthy competition can also push some providers into riskier asset segments.

2.7 Presentation of the Diagnostic Results

The country diagnostic reports begin by presenting findings on the broad public sector DRF landscape, including related recommendations. The results of the diagnostic analysis are then presented and finally summarized in a spider diagram depicting country scoring for each of the six areas of relevance for the development of a strong enabling environment for disaster

Figure: W&W Insurance, Reinsurance, and Capital Market Solutions Development Framework—Hypothetical Example

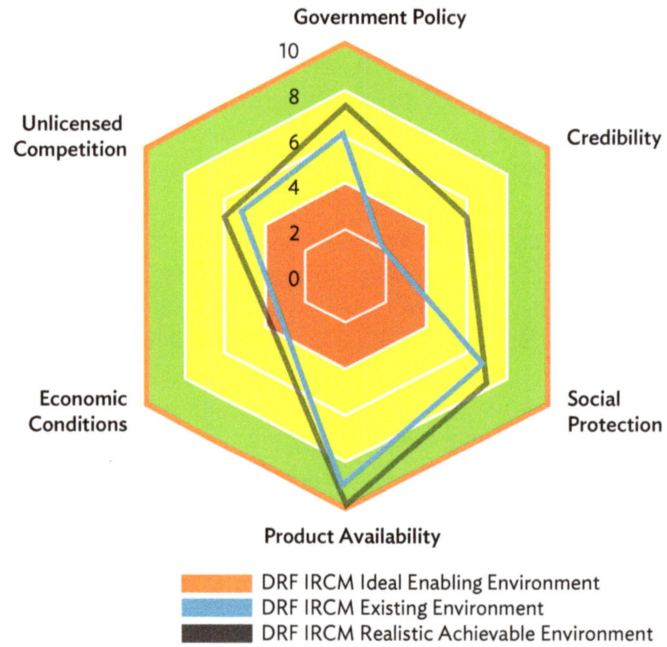

DRF= disaster risk financing; IRCM= insurance, reinsurance, and capital market.
Source: Asian Development Bank.

as well as epidemic and pandemic IRCM solutions (as demonstrated in the figure above). For each axis, an ideal enabling environment, a realistic environment, and the current state of the environment are depicted.

The ideal enabling conditions for the development of IRCM solutions for each of the six areas are defined. The assessors define this environment based on international good practice and expert judgment. This step considers the political, cultural, and religious contexts of the marketplace as well as international best practices.

A reality check defines the next best IRCM solutions enabling environment that can be achieved. The ideal enabling environment may be very difficult to achieve in practice, so a realistic enabling environment for each of the six areas is also determined on a country-by-country basis. This is the best achievable enabling environment and is developed drawing on local expertise gained through extensive stakeholder consultation and analysis of the questionnaires to identify likely impediments to achieving the ideal enabling environment. The ideal and realistic enabling environments will not necessarily differ significantly, resulting in that case in their overlap.

The current environment is then populated. Using local expertise and comments from relevant national stakeholders, including government authorities, private sector providers, and professional bodies, the current environment for each of the axes is determined.

The methodology used thus depicts the gaps between the current enabling environment for disaster IRCM solutions and the ideal and realistic alternatives. Comparison enables ready identification of areas for action, leading to the development of a strategy and road map to remove the gaps. The prioritization of actions to address the gaps should be based on the scale of the gap and reflect reasonable timeframes for completion. Urgent actions are recommended to strengthen the enabling environment in the areas of relevance, achieving scores of four or below (color red); medium-term actions are recommended for scores between four and six (yellow), and no immediate actions are required for higher scores (green). Where the realistic enabling environment differs from the ideal scenario, that difference between the existing and the realistic scenario rather than between the existing and the ideal scenario is considered when determining the urgency of the needed actions. The absolute scores have no further meaning and should not be used for cross-country comparisons.

3

Critical Opportunities to Enhance the Enabling Environment for Disaster Risk Financing

The comprehensive country diagnostics framework methodology was piloted in four countries (Fiji, Nepal, Pakistan, and Sri Lanka) and used in four other countries (Cambodia, Kyrgyz Republic, Pakistan, and the Philippines),[4] including financing response to pandemics and epidemics, highlighting several common opportunities to strengthen the enabling environment for IRCM solutions. The assessed countries represent a large diversity with respect to government structure, economy, disaster risk, population, geography, and the development of their financial sectors. This diversity was reflected in wide-ranging recommendations under each of the six axes of relevance for the development of disaster IRCM solutions. Nevertheless, several common actions for strengthening the enabling environment were also identified. It is expected that similar actions would benefit other countries.

Government policy in the development of risk transfer instruments for disaster risk financing:

- Develop a comprehensive register of all government-owned infrastructure and other assets, including regularly updated replacement values.
- Assess the current state of disaster risk modeling and mapping and implement actions to ensure comprehensive disaster risk modeling and mapping with sufficient granularity detail to support the development of an effective DRF strategy. Probabilistic modeling and analytical tools such as exceedance probability curves are valuable for assessing pandemic risk and estimating the potential burden of pandemics.
- Develop a national DRF strategy following the risk-layering approach.
- Consider introducing an agricultural insurance pool or improving the current functioning of the main provider.
- Consider a mandatory disaster insurance program for residential property.
- Consider business interruption insurance for the government in case of pandemics or severe epidemics.

Economic conditions and other support functions:

- Improve the economy and raise the population's purchasing power so that insurance becomes more affordable.
- Develop risk information infrastructure, e.g., forecasting capabilities, automated weather stations.
- Develop a data basis, e.g., exposure and loss data for disasters.

[4] Pakistan was assessed only on the enabling environment for financing instruments of pandemic or epidemic risk during the second phase of the technical assistance.

Disaster risk product availability and affordability:

- Expand the range of retail insurance products available for disaster protection.
- Develop new agricultural insurance products, such as hybrid agriculture insurance products combining indemnity-based and index-based coverage and comprehensive crop production and insurance solutions, supporting access to inputs, production advice, marketing services, and insurance.
- Develop pandemic and severe epidemic insurance products that go beyond medical protection, e.g., business interruption, travel insurance, etc.
- Develop mandatory environmental liability insurance.
- Explore opportunities to introduce ILS, including catastrophe bonds as DRF instruments.

Credibility of the private sector offering risk transfer solutions:

- Develop a customized insurance awareness program for disaster insurance.
- Increase underwriting capacity and risk management of insurance professionals (actuaries, auditors, reinsurance underwriters) involved in disaster insurance.
- Assess the insurance sector against the International Association of Insurance Supervisors Insurance Core Principles and standards and implement the required changes to enhance its credibility.

Social protection policy and tools:

- Develop a comprehensive strategy combining social protection of households below the poverty line through social insurance with innovative microinsurance products and through commercial insurance providers for households above the poverty line.
- Conduct a comprehensive review of national digital infrastructure to enhance seamless and cost-effective digital payment systems. This can create opportunities for public–private partnerships in the digital space.
- Consider creating public–private partnerships with the insurance industry to increase transparency, speed, and efficiency of social protection schemes.

Competition to the formal sector from informal and unlicensed providers:

- Develop microinsurance regulations to support the development of a regulated and vibrant microinsurance sector.
- Develop a proportionate regulatory framework for insurance providers that are not insurers (microfinance networks, farmers' cooperatives) and supervise them.
- Improve access to offshore insurance and capital markets for risk transfer cover that the local market cannot provide.

Sovereign disaster risk retention findings:

- The identified gaps and opportunities in sovereign disaster risk retention instruments are fully considered in the evaluation of the pertinent axis, and the corresponding recommendations are provided.

APPENDIX 1

Assessment of the State of Sovereign Disaster (Including Epidemic and Pandemic) Risk Financing Coverage—Questions for the Ministries of Finance

The questions below extracted from *Assessing Financial Protection against Disasters: A Guidance Note on Conducting a Disaster Risk Finance Diagnostic*, a 2017 report jointly prepared by the Asian Development Bank and the World Bank, are enhanced to include pandemic and epidemic risk financing considerations.

The questions are concise, but it is recognized that actual situations involve varying degrees of complexity. Respondents are encouraged to provide more detailed, comprehensive answers to the extent that they believe this is required to convey clear understanding.

1 Assessment of Fiscal Shocks Associated with Disasters

1. Concerning contingent liability of the government:[1]
   a. What are the government's legal, stated contingent liabilities associated with disasters (public assets, low-income housing, guarantees, etc.)?
      - **Accountant General:** Does the government have a centralized register of contingent liabilities?
      - **Accountant General**: If not, how are contingent liabilities tracked?
      - **Accountant General/Budgeting:** Does the federal/national government have full visibility on contingent liabilities at nonfederal or subnational domain?
      - **Accountant General:** How are contingent liabilities classified and subclassified?

   b. Historically, what implicit (i.e., socially/economically enforced) contingent liabilities has the government assumed (i.e., approved expenditure for) in the event of a disaster?
      - **Accountant General:** How are contingent liabilities recognized and valued if the government has not implemented the International Public Sector Accounting Standards (IPSAS) 19?

   c. How much has the government spent annually on post-disaster response over the past 10 years or other relevant period (ideally broken down according to humanitarian relief, early recovery, and reconstruction)?
      - **Auditor General:** Which parts of the Government Finance Statistics Manual 2014 chart has the government adopted within its line-item coding list?
      - **Auditor General:** Which administrative codes in the government chart of accounts relate to disaster risk financing (DRF) (to help identify spending and budgets)?
      - **Budgeting Division:** Which functional, programmatic or policy coding dimensions does the government use to classify DRF budgets and expenditures?

[1] Depending on the devolution of fiscal powers, the entire contingent liability is not of the federal government alone; provincial governments also have a share. This aspect needs to be clarified up front.

2. Concerning fiscal risk assessment of disaster shocks:
   a. Does the government have data on historical fiscal revenue loss because of disasters?
   b. Does the government have fiscal reserves for pandemics and epidemics? If so, what are these planned to cover (e.g., health versus economic costs)?
   c. How are losses estimated by the government and communicated to relevant authorities?
   d. What data, or categories of data, are included in these records?
   e. For how many years (and/or for how many disaster events) are records available?

3. Concerning public disclosure of disaster-related fiscal exposure:
   a. Does the government assess and disclose its fiscal exposure to disasters in its fiscal risk assessment, either voluntarily or because it is required to? If so,
   b. Does the government conduct this analysis by sector (e.g., agriculture, transport infrastructure, hydraulic infrastructure, education, health, etc.)?
   c. Does the government separately consider short-term and long-term fiscal risk from disasters?
   d. Does the government's fiscal planning take account of potential fiscal shocks related to disasters?
   e. Has the government identified any funding gaps in its post-disaster response (i.e., funding shortfall during relief, recovery, or reconstruction phases)?
   f. Does the government prebudget statement assess or report on fiscal exposure to disasters?
   g. Has the annual budget, medium-term budget, or other forecast document reported on fiscal exposure to disasters in the past 3 years?
   h. Did the finance minister refer to disaster risk fiscal exposure in the budget speech in the past 3 years?
   i. If the government has not implemented IPSAS 19, how does it report fiscal risk in relation to disasters? (When is the government expected to implement IPSAS 19?)
   j. Do participatory budgeting initiatives address disaster aspects on any level or to any extent?

2 Ex-Ante Disaster Risk Financing

1. Concerning the annual contingency budget:
   a. What portion of the government's annual national/federal appropriation is allocated to a contingency line for unforeseen events?
      - **Budgeting Division:** Is there an unallocated block in the annual appropriation?
      - **Budgeting Division/Accountant General/Auditor General:** How has this block allocation been used in recent years?
      - **Budgeting Division/Accountant General/Auditor General:** Is the unallocated block covered by policy or rules regarding use?
      - **Budgeting Division:** Does the budget call circular(s) reference disaster financing in the past 3 years?
   b. Do local governments (nonfederal/subnational domains) maintain annual contingency budgets?
      - **Local Government Ministry:** Do nonfederal/subnational governments have powers to establish contingencies or provisions for disaster response?
      - **Local Government Ministry:** How often is this power used?

- **Local Government Ministry/Budgeting Division:** Are sums reported to the federal/national government?
- **Local Government Ministry/Budgeting Division/Accountant General:** Is a summary register maintained?
- **Local Government Ministry:** Are conditional, matching, or special grants used to incentivize creation of contingencies or provisions?
- **Local Government Ministry:** Are conditional, matching, or special grants used to incentivize use of insurance premiums?
- **Local Government Ministry/Budgeting Division/Accountant General:** Does the Local Government Accounting Code recognize contingencies as envisaged by IPSAS 19?
- **Local Government Ministry/Budgeting Division/Accountant General:** Do local governments create contingencies or provisions?
- **Local Government Ministry/Budgeting Division/Accountant General:** Are local governments permitted to have unallocated blocks in their appropriations?
- **Local Government Ministry/Budgeting Division/Accountant General:** Does this happen often?

c. Are allocations (value of budgets and classification of expenditure line items) prescribed by statute?
   - **Local Government Ministry:** Which conditional grants are in place in statute?
   - **Local Government Ministry:** Which other grants are in place for local governments (special grants, matching grants etc.) and are they used?
   - Which grants for what purposes and are they used?
   - **Local Government Ministry:** Does the formula for unconditional grant recognize disaster risk of the recipient authority?
   - Is there a fiscal commission or other independent body involved in determining allocations between domains of government? (If yes, is there a statutory basis that references disaster risk included somewhere within the allocation calculations?)

d. For what purposes can the block allocation resources be used (including any nondisaster-related purposes)?
   - **Budgeting Division:** Explain the process of transfers from the unallocated block.
   - **Budgeting Division:** Do virement rules specify disasters (and other purposes) as circumstances for transfer from the unallocated block?

e. Who manages/controls access to these budget lines?
   - **Budgeting Division:** Which ministry controls the unallocated block? (Is it classified at the government level or are there ministry-level allocations?)
   - **Budgeting Division:** Is there a limit on transfers from the unallocated block?
   - **Budgeting Division:** If disasters are referenced specifically within the virement rules, how much can be used for this purpose?

f. Who can access them?
   - **Auditor General/Budgeting Divisions:** Which rules govern the use of the unallocated block?
   - **Budgeting Division:** Are there any purposes prescribed or excluded?

g. Typically, how long does it take for allocations from the contingency budget to be approved and disbursed?
   - **Budgeting Division:** When have transfers for the unallocated block been requested for disasters in recent years?
   - **Budgeting Division:** When (and to where) were transfers agreed?

h. Historically (say over the past 10 or 15 years), what is the longest period it has taken for all allocations from the contingency budget to be approved and disbursed?
i. Can any remaining funding be rolled over across budget years?
j. Please provide data on actual use of the national/federal contingency budget over the past 5 years (or another relevant period).
k. How is local revenue (in health and local government) treated within the appropriation system?
   - **Budgeting Division:** Are these entities allowed to retain these sums?
   - **Budgeting Division:** Are they accounted for and reported to the national and/or federal government?
   - **Budgeting Division:** Are these sums used to create reserves by the local entities?

2. Is there a dedicated budget line for disaster risk reduction (as opposed to a contingency line for disasters, which was covered under question 1)?
   a. **Budgeting Division**: Which lines in the appropriation are expected to be used in the event of a disaster (apart from the unallocated block)?
   b. **Budgeting Division**: Do line ministries have any dedicated resource provided for this purpose?
   c. **Budgeting Division**: If yes, which economic line items are used to identify the sums?

3. Is there a dedicated budget line for pandemic and health emergency preparedness? What is this intended to cover?

4. Is there a dedicated budget line for disaster risk reduction in the agriculture sector? If yes, which government agency is responsible for budget allocations for managing disaster risks in the agriculture sector?

5. Concerning a dedicated disaster reserve fund:
   a. **Accountant General:** Does the government maintain a disaster preparedness fund?
      - How is the fund financed?
      - What have been the main sources of income receipts to the fund?
      - Does the fund have specific powers?
      - How often and for what purposes has the fund been used in the past 10 years?
   b. If so, are funds held at the federal level or the provincial level?
      - Is the fund managed by a line ministry or by another type of organization with its own board and act of incorporation?
   c. Please indicate the current balance at each level.
      - Obtain copies of budgets, accounts, and audit reports for the fund.
   d. What amounts have been allocated to this fund over the last 5 years, and from what source(s) (e.g., government budget, private donations, and development partners)?
   e. For what purposes can the fund be used (e.g., disaster risk reduction, preparedness, relief, early recovery, reconstruction)?
      - Obtain mandate and act of incorporation of the fund.
      - Is the mandate adequate for purpose?
   f. Historically (say over the past 10 or 15 years), how often has this fund been exhausted at or before the end of the year?
   g. Please provide data on actual use of the fund over the past 5 years (or another relevant period).

6. Concerning line agency funding:
    a. Do line ministries (especially agriculture) have a dedicated budget line for disasters?
    b. Are related budget allocations prescribed by statute?
    c. For what purposes can the funds be used (e.g., risk reduction, preparedness, relief, early recovery, reconstruction [not only earthquake or flood-related disasters])?

7. Concerning contingent credit:
    a. Does the government use any contingent credit instruments for disaster response purposes?
    b. If so, what are typical terms, conditions, and loan periods (including trigger type/level) of these instruments?
    c. What are the return periods of the events that these funds are designed to cover?
    d. Have the contingent credit instruments ever been triggered? If so, please indicate the year or years and the amount of funding accessed on each occasion.

8. Concerning insurance for public assets, does the government purchase any disaster insurance for public assets? If so,
    a. Are line ministries and local governments legally required to purchase insurance for their public assets? If so, are they required to purchase cover based on replacement value?
        - **Accountant General:** Does the government or local government operate asset registers?
        - **Accountant General:** How are assets valued?
        - **Accountant General:** Which assets are included in the asset register (and which are not)?
        - **Auditor General/Accountant General:** Is the asset register checked and updated regularly?
        - Has the Auditor General made any comments or reports on completeness of asset registers?
        - **Accountant General:** Do boards within government control their own asset portfolios? (Explore their practices—do they have registers, balance sheets, insurance, etc.)
    b. Also identify which public assets are insured?
        - **Accountant General:** Is there a central register of insured assets?
    c. Is there any insurance of assets of state-owned enterprises (SOEs) and boards?
        - Which SOE report on an International Financial Reporting Standards basis with a balance sheet?
        - Can these entities identify their fixed assets with valuations as reported on the balance sheets?
        - Obtain copies of annual accounts of a selection of SOEs.
        - Do they use insurance products for their assets?
    d. If so, who is responsible for purchasing insurance (i.e., are risks pooled and insured aggregately or insured by individual managers)?
    e. Who is responsible for underwriting these types of insurance covers?
    f. If insurance is purchased for public assets, how is the transaction carried out? Is it through bidding? Or some other mechanism?
        - **Head of Procurement Agency:** How many procuring entities are there in the public sector?

- **Head of Procurement Agency:** Do entities freely associate for the purpose of procuring insurance? (Can they procure individually or in groups or is there a central policy—how does it work?)
- **Head of Procurement Agency:** How is public insurance procured?
- **Head of Procurement Agency:** Is the procurement of insurance required to be included in procurement plans? (Is it included in practice?)

g. Is there any central entity that coordinates purchase of cover and provides line ministries and local governments with technical assistance in this regard?
   - **Head of Procurement Agency/Line Ministries/SOEs/Boards/Local Government:** What advice is available to procuring entities regarding insurance?

h. What are the current amounts of insurance cover, premium rates, and associated premium payments? Are data available on specific assets insured?

9. Concerning other insurance, does the government purchase any other forms of insurance (e.g., sovereign parametric cover)? If so,
   a. Who is responsible for purchasing cover?
      - Refer to procurement questions above.
   b. How is the transaction carried out? Is it through bidding? Or some other mechanism?
      - Refer to procurement questions above.
   c. Please provide some examples of terms (including triggers) and amount of the cover?

10. Concerning risk transfer through capital markets, does the government utilize any capital market instruments to transfer risk directly to the capital markets (e.g., catastrophe bonds)? If so,
    a. Who is responsible for purchasing cover?
    b. What are the terms (including triggers) and amount of the cover?

3 Ex-Post Disaster Risk Financing

1. Concerning Treasury Management:
   a. **Treasury/Accountant General:** How does the government ensure that cash is available to response entities to draw for disaster purposes?
   b. **Treasury/Accountant General:** Are banks used for liquidity in the process?
   c. **Treasury Management:** Is authority to spend and overspend issued during disaster response? (How quickly and to which entities? Is this dependent on the point of the financial year?)

2. Concerning accounting for disaster expenditures:
   a. **Accountant General:** Does the government use the same chart of accounts to classify expenditures incurred in disaster response as in normal circumstances?
   b. **Accountant General:** How can expenditures related to a specific disaster be identified and reported? (Is a reserved policy or programmatic dimension used from the chart of accounts for this purpose?)

3. Concerning post-disaster budget reallocation:
   a. Are there any regulations or other formal constraints regarding reallocations within existing budget lines at the discretion of the budget line holder (e.g., a line agency), including any limits on amounts?

- Are temporary reallocations (virements) reversed post-event?
- Where does the power and responsibility lie for deciding which budgets to reallocate within the line agencies and local government? (Or is this purely a matter for the Ministry of Finance?)
- Are reallocations/virements specifically identified with events?

b. Are there any regulations or other formal constraints (including approval processes) regarding reallocation between budget lines and government agencies, including any limits on amounts?

c. Typically, how long does it take to pass a supplementary budget and, if such budgets can be passed only according to fixed schedules, how often and when can they be passed?

d. Are historical data on the scale of post-disaster reallocations readily available and, if so, from where?
   - Are reallocations recorded and reversed?

e. Has the government faced any major hurdles or delays in determining and approving post-disaster budget reallocations?

4. Concerning external assistance:

   a. How much external assistance has been provided in response to recent disaster events (over the past 10 years or another relevant period)? Please provide data for each relevant disaster event and donors involved, if available.

   b. **International Cooperation Division:** What proportion of this assistance has been in the form of (i) grants; (ii) loans; and (iii) technical assistance?

   c. Approximately what portion of the disaster response financing has been provided by international assistance?
      - **Accountant General:** Does the chart of accounts have a dimension to track expenditure by source of funds (e.g., by donor or government, conditional grant, etc.)?

   d. What portion of external assistance is typically targeted directly at beneficiaries in the form of cash transfers or in-kind assistance?

   e. What are the targeting mechanisms through which cash or in-kind assistance is delivered to beneficiaries?

   f. What are the delivery mechanisms for cash transfers (e.g., the payment mechanisms of existing social protection programs) or in-kind assistance?
      - Is the banking system used in distributing cash to beneficiaries during a disaster?
      - Is mobile money used to transfer directly to beneficiaries?
      - Does local or central/federal government authorize cash payments to beneficiaries?
      - How is the liability calculated and who is responsible for the calculation? (Are there rules in place based on household numbers or something similar?)
      - Are existing social protection programs used in a disaster to distribute funding or are separate arrangements in place?
      - How is the payment authorized?
      - How is receipt of the payment acknowledged?
      - Is a separate dimension within the chart of accounts used to identify disaster-specific expenditure?

5. Concerning other ex-post mechanisms (over the past 10 years or another relevant period):
   a. Are there cases of ex-gratia relief from national relief funds to provincial governments?
      - Which funds and mechanisms were used to finance and facilitate transfers to nonfederal government institutions?
   b. What other ex-post financing sources has the government used to finance disaster response (e.g., domestic and/or external borrowing, tax increases, etc.)?
      - **Tax authority:** Is a central register of taxes maintained?
      - **Tax authority**: Does each (new) tax have a separate code in the chart of accounts?
      - **Debt Management Unit**: Which loans and from which lender(s)[2] has the government borrowed for disaster response? (Or is borrowing generally for general support for a deficit?)
   c. How much financing has each relevant mechanism generated each time it has been used?
   d. Approximately what portion of the disaster response financing has each relevant source provided?

4 Post-Disaster Expenditure

1. Are historical data available regarding government expenditure on post-disaster relief, early recovery, and reconstruction (not only earthquake and flood but also drought, tsunami, and other type of natural hazards)?

2. Are there historical data (including data from the recent COVID-19 outbreak) on the costs of post-pandemic/epidemic expenditure (ideally broken down by costs of new health-care infrastructure and equipment and cost of economic measures)?

3. Are there specific sectors that have been/would be disproportionately affected by pandemics and epidemics (e.g., tourism, manufacturing, etc.)?

5 Scrutiny

1. **Auditor General:** Are audit plans for the performance of disaster response or disaster arrangements in line with the International Standards of Supreme Audit Institutions 5520 (https://www.issai.org/wp-content/uploads/2019/08/issai-5520-e.pdf)?

2. **Auditor General:** Are audit reports available?

3. **Auditor General/Accountant General:** Are separate disaster expenditure report formats specified in financial rules?

4. **Auditor General/Accountant General:** Which separate financial and activity reports were produced from past disasters?

[2] Domestic and international.

APPENDIX 2

Disaster Risk Financing—The Enabling Environment Questionnaire for Insurance, Reinsurance, and Capital Market Solutions

1 Axis: Government Policy

Respondents are asked to assess the current and realistic enabling environment against the ideal enabling environment for each of the factors listed in the table below.

Current Environment	Realistic Enabling Environment	Ideal Enabling Environment
		Declared government policy on insurance, reinsurance, and capital market (IRCM) solutions *(Please describe the state of government policy supporting the development of IRCM solutions.)* *When responding to this question, please consider the various sectors affected by disasters as different sectors may have different protection policies. Please cover at least the following: sovereign protection, agriculture (crop and livestock) protection, private sector protection in general, and low-income population protection.*
		Well-coordinated institutional arrangements for the application of IRCM solutions across relevant government ministries and agencies, including local government entities
		Well-complemented and coordinated roles of relevant government ministries and agencies on IRCM policy declaration and execution
		Customized regulation or other formal guidance of IRCM solutions
		Effective liability laws in place
		Effective financial literacy programs resulting in a high level of financial literacy in the population
		Tax incentives for the use of IRCM solutions
		Tax incentives for providers of IRCM solutions
		Tax-free premiums
		Premium subsidies
		Financial aid for commercially uninsurable risks
		Mandatory health-care cover for the population, either through direct government provision or the use of a social health insurance scheme
		Social health program sustainability regularly evaluated by an actuary or a similar expert
		Coverage for pandemics/epidemics under government-provided health-care schemes and/or social health insurance

continued on next page

Table *continued*

Current Environment	Realistic Enabling Environment	Ideal Enabling Environment
		Effective border control policies, including border health teams to screen for signs of communicable disease (e.g., temperature checking machines, health declarations, etc.)
		Strict policies governing animal–human interactions, including but not limited to wet markets and wildlife trade Strong regulator in place that takes enforcement action and has a track record of prosecutions
		Policies and procedures in place for pandemic/epidemic emergency preparedness including plans to limit contagion risks, plans for health-care infrastructure use and stockpiling
		Robust policies for public health, particularly communicable disease control
		Robust and well-coordinated public health messaging, resulting in a high level of population health literacy, particularly as it pertains to hygiene, sanitation, and the management of communicable disease

In completing the above table, please address the following items:

1. What is the government's policy and involvement regarding agricultural insurance? For example, does it offer
   a. insurance education? If yes, how is it offered (e.g., informational session, seminars, web/tv/radio communication, advisory services)?
   b. subsidies for crop and livestock insurance? If yes, what types of subsidies are provided (e.g., premium, claim, financing loss assessment)?
   c. negotiated lower rates for agricultural insurance? Who is setting the premium rates for crop and livestock insurance (e.g., insurance companies, government, insurance regulator, etc.)?

2. Is there a law (or any other legislative document) on agricultural insurance?

3. Does the government impose special requirements to agricultural insurers or insurance companies offering crop and livestock insurance?

4. Insurance regulator: Is agricultural insurance a separate type of insurance or a separate risk class or is it reported within property insurance? Do the insurance companies report separately on crop and livestock insurance?

5. What is the objective of the subsidized agricultural insurance program (e.g., cost of production recovery, support for farmers' income, increase commodity production, introduction of new farming practices and/or technologies)?

6. Does the government view agricultural insurance as an expected means by which financing institutions will
   a. defray agricultural loans?
   b. reduce default risk on agricultural loans?
   c. reduce the cost of credit?

7. What are the respective roles of central and provincial governments in the IRCM market regarding
   a. claims settlement?
   b. grievance redress?
   c. premium subsidy
      - nature (paid to commercial or government-owned insurer/s)?
      - scale (as % of premium)?
      - relative outlay (as % of annual government expense)?
   d. rate making and negotiation?
   e. making risk transfer products available?
   f. advertising and provision of additional information to support agricultural insurance?

8. What is the government's policy and degree of support regarding ex-post loss and coping mechanisms? For example, the latest evidence (e.g., for the past 5 years) on compensation and relief to farmers. Is this data available per disaster type?

2 Axis: Economic Conditions and Other Support Functions

Respondents are requested to assess the current and realistic enabling environment against the ideal enabling environment for each of the factors listed in the table below.

Current Environment	Realistic Enabling Environment	Ideal Enabling Environment
		Growing economy
		Manageable inflation
		Access to financial services
		Availability of affordable credit
		No foreign exchange and withholding tax (including permanent establishment) restrictions that could stymie (re)insurance transactions
		Well-developed extension services for agriculture and livestock insurance, health insurance, etc.
		Business continuity requirements for the insurance and capital market sectors
		Liquid and developed capital market, including a liquid secondary market
		Promotion of disaster risk reduction
		Comprehensive disaster risk data
		Readily accessible meteorological and geophysical data and weather forecasts
		Readily accessible agricultural production data
		Effective crop protection and veterinary services
		Professional financial services, including auditing

continued on next page

Table *continued*

Current Environment	Realistic Enabling Environment	Ideal Enabling Environment
		Strong government technical disaster risk management capacity
		An established regulatory body for pharmaceuticals with expedited processes for approving emergency-use therapies
		High levels of clinical training, particularly in disease detection, to enable outbreaks to be effectively diagnosed and reported
		Containment facilities, either in hospitals or other suitable locations, specifically designed for infectious patients/ disease outbreaks
		A high degree of multilateral cooperation with entities such as the World Health Organization (WHO) to coordinate global pandemics and epidemics
		Hospital beds to population ratio is near the Organisation for Economic Co-operation and Development (OECD) average
		Doctor to population ratio is near OECD average
		Nurse to population ratio is near OECD average
		Sufficient critical equipment (CT scanners, MRI scanners, ventilators) to cope with existing demand and surge demand during a pandemic
		Nonhealth-care workers in frontline caregiving roles (e.g., social services, social workers, nursing home staff) trained in infection control and management
		Sufficient cold storage capacity across the country to cope with routine and surge demand (e.g., mass vaccination under a pandemic)
		Strong vaccination uptake rates for routine vaccinations (e.g., Measles, Mumps, and Rubella) and literacy among the population for vaccines

3 Axis: Product Availability and Affordability

Respondents are asked to assess the current and realistic enabling environment against the ideal enabling environment for each of the factors listed in the table below.

Current Environment	Realistic Enabling Environment	Ideal Enabling Environment
		Wide range of disaster insurance products available *(Please provide an overview of the existing disaster insurance and capital market solutions available. If possible, the overview should include an indication of the level of usage of each product in the form of premium volume and number of policies compared with the potential buyers.)*
		Consumer-centered development of products
		No unnecessary, compulsory add-ons to the disaster insurance products

continued on next page

Table *continued*

Current Environment	Realistic Enabling Environment	Ideal Enabling Environment
		Affordability for the targeted consumers
		Convenient distribution channels
		Ease of premium payments including premium financing
		Appropriate speed of claims payments
		No unreasonable exclusions
		Religious and cultural aspects reflected in product design
		Incentives for purchase of disaster risk financing products
		Mandatory insurance for extreme disaster risks
		Mandatory international reinsurance or retrocession for extreme disaster risks
		Capital market solutions such as catastrophic bonds available to transfer disaster risk *(Please describe any existing capital market products that are used by insurers or the government to transfer disaster risks. If those instruments are not yet available, please provide information on any initiative in this area.)*
		Business continuity insurance covers not excluding pandemics/epidemics
		Loss of income due to pandemics/epidemics such as inability to fulfill orders, shipping, etc. Mandatory slaughtering of infected animals, etc.
		Private health insurance products (including reimbursement plans and critical illness plans) that are commercially available, cover pandemic/epidemic risks
		Crop and livestock insurance products available (indemnity, index-based) (multiple and/or named perils)
		Insurance cover basis—cost of production, market value of commodities, revenue/income protection
		Specific requirements for subsidized agricultural insurance products
		Mandatory or voluntary crop and livestock insurance products or perils to be insured
		Loss adjustment for agricultural insurance done by independent experts, experts employed by insurance companies, or government agency staff
		Agricultural insurance products offered by • insurers • agents • brokers • finance institutions • agribusiness companies • traders and processors • others

4 Axis: Credibility of Insurance and Capital Market Stakeholders

Respondents are asked to assess the current and realistic enabling environment against the ideal enabling environment for each of the factors listed in the table below.

Current Environment	Realistic Enabling Environment	Ideal Enabling Environment
		Reputable regulator overseeing modern insurance and capital market supervisory legislation *(Please provide an estimate of the level of compliance with the International Association of Insurance Supervisors and the International Organization of Securities Commissions principles and standards.)*
		Well-established and credible insurance and capital markets *(Please provide an overview of the insurance and capital markets with respect to the regulation and key market statistics.)*
		A solvent insurance market *(Please provide an overview of the solvency, risk management, and risk transfer requirements for insurers.)*
		Reliable rating agencies *(Please provide an overview of the rating agencies operating in the country, including whether they include internationally accepted agencies or local ones only.)*
		Active press reporting on insurance and capital markets
		Use of high-quality reinsurers and reinsurance brokers *(Please provide an overview of the legal requirements applicable to reinsurers and reinsurance brokers.)*
		Confidence in and an impeccable image of the insurance sector
		Confidence in and an impeccable image of the capital markets
		A fair pricing culture
		A fair claims payment culture
		Contracts capable of being enforced within a reliable judicial system
		Trained and ethical agents/brokers and reinsurance brokers
		Adequate availability of all insurance experts (actuaries, brokers, risk assessors, financial advisors, loss adjustors)
		Accessible and effective complaints and redress mechanisms in place for insurance and capital market transactions
		Transparent costs of available insurance, reinsurance, and capital market solutions
		Available products easily understood by targeted consumers
		No misleading advertisement
		Guarantee fund for insolvencies of insurers and broker–dealers

5 Axis: Social Protection Policy

Respondents are requested to assess the current and realistic enabling environment against the ideal enabling environment for each of the factors listed in the table below.

Current Environment	Realistic Enabling Environment	Ideal Enabling Environment
		An effective social protection strategy that includes insurance, reinsurance, and capital market (IRCM) solutions *(Please describe the current social protection strategy of the government. This should include all social insurance programs in place, the mode of execution, and some performance indicators.)*
		Provision of social protection only for risks that cannot be transferred to the private sector either as insurance, reinsurance, or capital market solutions
		An existing analysis of risks that can be transferred to the private sector to increase effectiveness and manage budgetary costs and implementation of its findings
		Cost equivalence for any similar protection products provided both by the government and the private sector
		No carving out risks necessary for IRCM solutions to be sustainable (In commercial insurance, there is often cross-subsidy between different risks covered. Carving out of the risks that support the cost of covering less commercially attractive risks would reduce the viability of insurance.)
		Targeted post-disaster public support for poor households only (Full public support for all affected households would bring into question the necessity of private insurance.)
		Government support for affected public due to pandemics or epidemics
		Available social assistance products not crowding out IRCM solutions *(Please describe the social assistance that is provided to agricultural and low-income populations, including conditional cash transfer programs for low-income populations, minimum crop support prices for seeds, fertilizer subsidies, etc.)*
		Initiatives under implementation to promote microinsurance and Takaful insurance
		Robust and well-regulated health insurance market complimenting public provision
		Shock-responsive social protection schemes duly in place to quickly cover poor people and those who fall into poverty/informality because of pandemic-induced economic downturn (schemes sufficiently financed, able to respond quickly, enabling database of beneficiaries and efficient payout mechanisms in place)

6 Axis: Competition to the Formal Sector from Informal and Unlicensed Providers

Respondents are asked to assess the current and realistic enabling environment against the ideal enabling environment for each of the factors listed in the table below.

Current Environment	Realistic Enabling Environment	Ideal Enabling Environment
		Enforced regulation of unlicensed insurance and capital market activity
		All health insurance providers regulated by the insurance supervisor
		Viability of hospital and other health assistance plans evaluated by an actuary or similar expert
		All agriculture insurance providers regulated by the insurance supervisor
		Agriculture assistance plans that promise future benefits in exchange of a fee evaluated by technical people
		Public awareness programs on the potential dangers of using unlicensed insurance providers
		Solvency requirements regarding unlicensed activity and the existence of a modern law to cover insolvencies of financial institutions, including insurers
		Regulation of cross-border insurance, reinsurance, and capital markets (IRCMs) to avoid regulatory arbitrage
		Brokers, national and foreign, operating under a level regulatory environment
		National and foreign reinsurers and insurers operating under a level regulatory environment
		Premium discounting and rebating regulation
		Technical pricing requirements
		No monopoly for the provision of IRCM solutions
		Law mandating that property or agriculture risks should be insured with licensed insurers
		Equal taxation for equivalent products, independent of provider
		Licensed and regulated health providers

APPENDIX 3

Assessment of the State of Sovereign Epidemic and Pandemic Risk Financing Coverage—Questions for the Ministries of Finance

The questions below are adapted from *Assessing Financial Protection Against Disasters: A Guidance Note on Conducting a Disaster Risk Finance Diagnostic*, a 2017 report jointly prepared by the Asian Development Bank and the World Bank.

The questions are concise, but it is recognized that actual situations involve varying degrees of complexity. Respondents are encouraged to provide more detailed, comprehensive answers to the extent that they believe this is required to convey clear understanding.

1 Assessment of Fiscal Shocks Associated with Epidemics and Pandemics

1. Concerning contingent liability of the government:[1]
   a. What are the government's legal, stated contingent liabilities associated with epidemics/pandemics (health-related costs, livelihood support, economic reactivation grants, etc.)?
      - **Accountant General:** Does the government have a centralized register of contingent liabilities?
      - **Accountant General**: If not, how are contingent liabilities tracked?
      - **Accountant General/Budgeting**: Does the federal/national government have full visibility on contingent liabilities at nonfederal or subnational domain?
      - **Accountant General**: How are contingent liabilities classified and subclassified?
   b. Historically, what implicit (i.e., socially/economically enforced) contingent liabilities has the government assumed (i.e., approved expenditure for) in the event of epidemics/pandemics?
      - **Accountant General**: How are contingent liabilities recognized and valued if the Government has not implemented the International Public Sector Accounting Standards (IPSAS) 19?
   c. How much has the government spent annually on post- epidemics/pandemics response over the past 10 years or other relevant period (ideally broken down according to humanitarian relief, economic support and recovery, and infrastructure upgrading)?
      - **Auditor General:** Which parts of the Government Finance Statistics Manual 2014 chart has the government adopted within its line-item coding list?
      - **Auditor General**: Which administrative codes in the government chart of accounts relate to epidemic/pandemic risk financing (to help identify spending and budgets)?
      - **Budgeting Division:** Which functional, programmatic or policy coding dimensions does the government use to classify epidemic/pandemic risk financing budgets and expenditures?

[1] Depending on the devolution of fiscal powers, the entire contingent liability is not of the federal government alone; provincial governments also have a share. This aspect needs to be clarified upfront.

2. Concerning fiscal risk assessment of epidemic/pandemic shocks:
   a. Does the government have data on historical fiscal revenue loss because of epidemics/pandemics?
   b. Does the government have fiscal reserves for pandemics and epidemics? If so, what are these planned to cover (e.g., health versus economic costs)?
   c. How are losses estimated by the government and communicated to relevant authorities?
   d. What data, or categories of data, are included in these records?
   e. For how many years (and/or for how many epidemic/pandemic events) are records available?

3. Concerning public disclosure of epidemic- or pandemic-related fiscal exposure:
   a. Does the government assess and disclose its fiscal exposure to epidemics/pandemics in its fiscal risk assessment, either voluntarily or because it is required to? If so,
   b. Does the government conduct this analysis by affected sector (e.g., agriculture, tourism, small and medium-sized enterprises, education, health, etc.)?
   c. Does the government separately consider short-term and long-term fiscal risk from epidemics/pandemics?
   d. Does the government's fiscal planning take account of potential fiscal shocks related to epidemics/pandemics?
   e. Has the government identified any funding gaps in its post-epidemic or post-pandemic response (i.e., funding shortfall during relief, recovery, or upgrading phases)?
   f. Does the government prebudget statement assess or report on fiscal exposure to epidemics/pandemics?
   g. Has the annual budget, medium-term budget, or other forecast document reported on fiscal exposure to epidemics/pandemics in the past 3 years?
   h. Did the finance minister refer to epidemics/pandemics risk fiscal exposure in the budget speech in the past 3 years?
   i. If the government has not implemented IPSAS 19, how does it report fiscal risk in relation to epidemics/pandemics? (When is the government expected to implement IPSAS 19?)
   j. Do participatory budgeting initiatives address epidemics/pandemics aspects on any level or to any extent?

2 Ex-Ante Epidemic and Pandemic Risk Financing

1. Concerning the annual contingency budget:
   a. What portion of the government's annual national/federal appropriation is allocated to a contingency line for unforeseen events?
      - **Budgeting Division**: Is there an unallocated block in the annual appropriation?
      - **Budgeting Division/Accountant General/Auditor General**: How has this block allocation been used in recent years?
      - **Budgeting Division/Accountant General/Auditor General**: Is the unallocated block covered by policy or rules regarding use?
      - **Budgeting Division:** Does the budget call circular(s) reference epidemics/pandemics financing in the past 3 years?
   b. Do local governments (nonfederal/subnational domains) maintain annual contingency budgets?
      - **Local Government Ministry**: Do nonfederal/subnational governments have powers to establish contingencies or provisions for epidemics/pandemics response?
      - **Local Government Ministry**: How often is this power used?

- **Local Government Ministry/Budgeting Division**: Are sums reported to the federal/national government?
- **Local Government Ministry/Budgeting Division/Accountant General**: Is a summary register maintained?
- **Local Government Ministry:** Are conditional, matching, or special grants used to incentivize creation of contingencies or provisions?
- **Local Government Ministry:** Are conditional, matching, or special grants used to incentivize use of insurance premiums?
- **Local Government Ministry/Budgeting Division/Accountant General**: Does the Local Government Accounting Code recognize contingencies as envisaged by IPSAS 19?
- **Local Government Ministry/Budgeting Division/Accountant General**: Do local governments create contingencies or provisions?
- **Local Government Ministry/Budgeting Division/Accountant General**: Are local governments permitted to have unallocated blocks in their appropriations?
- **Local Government Ministry/Budgeting Division/Accountant General**: Does this happen often?

c. Are allocations (value of budgets and classification of expenditure line items) prescribed by statute?
   - **Local Government Ministry**: Which conditional grants are in place in statute?
   - **Local Government Ministry**: Which other grants are in place for local governments (special grants, matching grants, etc.) and are they used?
   - Which grants for what purposes and are they used?
   - **Local Government Ministry**: Does the formula for unconditional grant recognize epidemics/pandemics risk of the recipient authority?
   - Is there a fiscal commission or other independent body involved in determining allocations between domains of government? (If yes, is there a statutory basis that references epidemics/pandemics risk included somewhere within the allocation calculations?)

d. For what purposes can the block allocation resources be used (including any nonepidemic- or nonpandemic-related purposes)?
   - **Budgeting Division:** Explain the process of transfers from the unallocated block.
   - **Budgeting Division:** Do virement rules specify epidemics/pandemics (and other purposes) as circumstances for transfer from the unallocated block?

e. Who manages/controls access to these budget lines?
   - **Budgeting Division:** Which ministry controls the unallocated block? (Is it classified at the government level or are there ministry-level allocations?)
   - **Budgeting Division:** Is there a limit on transfers from the unallocated block?
   - **Budgeting Division:** If epidemics/pandemics are referenced specifically within the virement rules, how much can be used for this purpose?

f. Who can access them?
   - **Auditor General/Budgeting Divisions**: Which rules govern the use of the unallocated block?
   - **Budgeting Division:** Are there any purposes prescribed or excluded?

g. Typically, how long does it take for allocations from the contingency budget to be approved and disbursed?
   - **Budgeting Division**: When have transfers for the unallocated block been requested for epidemics/pandemics in recent years?
   - **Budgeting Division**: When (and to where) were transfers agreed?

h. Historically (say over the past 10 or 15 years), what is the longest period it has taken for all allocations from the contingency budget to be approved and disbursed?
i. Can any remaining funding be rolled over across budget years?
j. Please provide data on actual use of the national/federal contingency budget over the past 5 years (or another relevant period).
k. How is local revenue (in health and local government) treated within the appropriation system?
    - **Budgeting Division**: Are these entities allowed to retain these sums?
    - **Budgeting Division**: Are they accounted for and reported to the national and/or federal government?
    - **Budgeting Division**: Are these sums used to create reserves by the local entities?

2. Is there a dedicated budget line for epidemics/pandemics risk reduction/prevention (as opposed to a contingency line for epidemics/pandemics, which was covered under question 1)?
    a. **Budgeting Division**: Which lines in the appropriation are expected to be used in the event of an epidemic/pandemic (apart from the unallocated block)?
    b. **Budgeting Division**: Do line ministries have any dedicated resources provided for this purpose?
    c. **Budgeting Division**: If yes, which economic line items are used to identify the sums?

3. Concerning a dedicated disaster (including epidemics/pandemics) reserve fund:
    a. **Accountant General:** Does the government maintain a disaster (including epidemics/pandemics) preparedness fund?
        - How is the fund financed?
        - What have been the main sources of income receipts to the fund?
        - Does the fund have specific powers?
        - How often and for what purposes has the fund been used in the past 10 years?
    b. If so, are funds held at the federal level or the provincial level?
        - Is the fund managed by a line ministry or by another type of organization with its own board and act of incorporation?
    c. Please indicate the current balance at each level.
        - Please attach/provide the links to copies of budgets, accounts, and audit reports for the fund.
    d. What amounts have been allocated to this fund over the last 5 years, and from what source(s) (e.g., government budget, private donations, and development partners)?
    e. For what purposes can the fund be used (e.g., disaster risk reduction, preparedness, relief, early recovery, reconstruction)?
        - Obtain mandate and act of incorporation of the fund.
        - Is the mandate adequate for purpose?
    f. Historically (say over the past 10 or 15 years), how often has this fund been exhausted at or before the end of the year?
    g. Please provide data on actual use of the fund over the past 5 years (or another relevant period).

4. Concerning line agency funding:
    a. Do line ministries (especially health) have a dedicated budget line for epidemics/pandemics?
    b. Are related budget allocations prescribed by statute?

c. For what purposes can the funds be used (e.g., risk reduction, preparedness, relief, early recovery, upgrading reconstruction)?

5. Concerning contingent credit:
   a. Does the government use any contingent credit instruments for epidemic/pandemic response purposes?
   b. If so, what are typical terms, conditions, and loan periods (including trigger type/level) of these instruments?
   c. What are the return periods of the events that these funds are designed to cover?
   d. Have the contingent credit instruments ever been triggered? If so, please indicate the year or years and the amount of funding accessed on each occasion.

6. Concerning insurance for hospitals and other health facilities, does the government purchase any insurance? If so,
   a. Are line ministries and local governments legally required to purchase insurance for their hospitals and other health facilities? If so, are they required to purchase cover based on replacement value?
      - **Accountant General:** Does the government or local government operate hospitals and other health facilities registers?
      - **Accountant General:** How are these assets valued?
      - **Accountant General:** Which of these assets are included in the asset register (and which are not)?
      - **Auditor General/Accountant General:** Is the asset register checked and updated regularly?
      - **Auditor General:** Has the Auditor General made any comments or reports on completeness of asset registers?
      - **Accountant General:** Do boards within government control their own asset portfolios? (Explore their practices. Do they have registers, balance sheets, insurance, etc.?)
      - **Accountant General:** Is there a central register of insured hospitals and other health facilities?
   b. Who is responsible for underwriting these types of insurance covers?
   c. If insurance is purchased for hospitals and other health facilities, how is the transaction carried out? Is it through bidding? Or some other mechanism?
      - **Head of Procurement Agency**: How many procuring entities are there in the public sector?
      - **Head of Procurement Agency:** Do entities freely associate for the purpose of procuring insurance? (Can they procure individually or in groups or is there a central policy? How does it work?)
      - **Head of Procurement Agency:** How is public insurance procured?
      - **Head of Procurement Agency:** Is the procurement of insurance required to be included in procurement plans? (Is it included in practice?)
   d. Is there any central entity that coordinates purchase of cover and provides line ministries and local governments with technical assistance in this regard?
      - **Head of Procurement Agency/Line Ministries/State-owned Enterprises/Boards/Local Government:** What advice is available to procuring entities regarding insurance?
   e. What are the current amounts of insurance cover, premium rates, and associated premium payments? Are data available on specific assets insured?

7. Concerning other insurance, does the government purchase any other forms of insurance against epidemics/pandemics (e.g., sovereign parametric cover)? If so,
   a. Who is responsible for purchasing cover?
      - Refer to procurement questions above.
   b. How is the transaction carried out? Is it through bidding? Or some other mechanism?
      - Refer to procurement questions above.
   c. Please provide some examples of terms (including triggers) and amount of the cover?

8. Concerning risk transfer through capital markets, does the government utilize any capital market instruments to transfer risk directly to the capital markets (e.g., epidemic/pandemic bonds)? If so,
   a. Who is responsible for purchasing cover?
   b. What are the terms (including triggers related to epidemics/pandemics) and amount of the cover?

3 Ex-Post Epidemic and Pandemic Risk Financing

1. Concerning Treasury Management:
   a. **Treasury/Accountant General:** How does the government ensure that cash is available to response entities to draw for epidemic/pandemic purposes?
   b. **Treasury/Accountant General:** Are banks used for liquidity in the process?
   c. **Treasury Management:** Is authority to spend and overspend issued during epidemic/pandemic response? (How quickly and to which entities? Is this dependent on the point of the financial year?)

2. Concerning accounting for epidemic/pandemic expenditures:
   a. **Accountant General:** Does the government use the same chart of accounts to classify expenditures incurred in epidemics/pandemics response as in normal circumstances?
   b. **Accountant General:** How can expenditures related to a specific epidemic/pandemic be identified and reported? (Is a reserved policy or programmatic dimension used from the chart of accounts for this purpose?)

3. Concerning post-epidemic/post-pandemic budget reallocation:
   a. Are there any regulations or other formal constraints regarding reallocations within existing budget lines at the discretion of the budget line holder (e.g., a line agency), including any limits on amounts?
      - Are temporary reallocations (virements) reversed post-event?
      - Where does the power and responsibility lie for deciding which budgets to reallocate within the line agencies and local government? (Or is this purely a matter for the Ministry of Finance?)
      - Are reallocations/virements specifically identified with events?
   b. Are there any regulations or other formal constraints (including approval processes) regarding reallocation between budget lines and government agencies, including any limits on amounts?
   c. Typically, how long does it take to pass a supplementary budget and, if such budgets can be passed only according to fixed schedules, how often and when can they be passed?
   d. Are historical data on the scale of post-epidemic/post-pandemic reallocations readily available and, if so, from where?
      - Are reallocations recorded and reversed?

   e. Has the government faced any major hurdles or delays in determining and approving post-epidemic/post-pandemic budget reallocations?

4. Concerning external assistance:
   a. How much external assistance has been provided in response to recent epidemic/pandemic events (over the past 10 years or another relevant period)? Please provide data for each relevant event and donors involved, if available.
   b. **International Cooperation Division:** What proportion of this assistance has been in the form of (i) grants; (ii) loans; and (iii) technical assistance?
   c. Approximately what portion of the epidemic/pandemic response financing has been provided by international assistance?
      - **Accountant General:** Does the chart of accounts have a dimension to track expenditure by source of funds (e.g., by donor or government, conditional grant, etc.)?
   d. What portion of external assistance is typically targeted directly at beneficiaries in the form of cash transfers or in-kind assistance?
   e. What are the targeting mechanisms through which cash or in-kind assistance is delivered to beneficiaries?
   f. What are the delivery mechanisms for cash transfers (e.g., the payment mechanisms of existing social protection programs) or in-kind assistance?
      - Is the banking system used in distributing cash to beneficiaries during an epidemic or a pandemic?
      - Is mobile money used to transfer directly to beneficiaries?
      - Does local or central/federal government authorize cash payments to beneficiaries?
      - How is the liability calculated and who is responsible for the calculation? (Are there rules in place based on household numbers or whatever?)
      - Are existing social protection programs used in an epidemic or a pandemic to distribute funding or are separate arrangements in place?
      - How is the payment authorized?
      - How is receipt of the payment acknowledged?
      - Is a separate dimension within the chart of accounts used to identify epidemic- or pandemic-specific expenditures?

5. Concerning other ex-post mechanisms (over the past 10 years or another relevant period):
   a. Are there cases of ex-gratia relief from national relief funds to provincial governments?
      - Which funds and mechanisms were used to finance and facilitate transfers to nonfederal government institutions?
   b. What other ex-post financing sources has the government used to finance epidemic/pandemic response (e.g., domestic and/or external borrowing, tax increases, etc.)?
      - **Tax authority:** Is a central register of taxes maintained?
      - **Tax authority**: Does each (new) tax have a separate code in the chart of accounts?
      - **Debt Management Unit**: Which loans and from which lender(s)[2] has the government borrowed for epidemic/pandemic response? (Or is borrowing generally for general support for a deficit?)
   c. How much financing has each relevant mechanism generated each time it has been used?
   d. Approximately what portion of the epidemic/pandemic response financing has each relevant source provided?

[2] Domestic and international.

4 Post-Epidemic and Post-Pandemic Expenditures

1. Are historical data available on the costs of post-epidemic/pandemic expenditures (ideally broken down by costs of health treatments including vaccines, new health-care infrastructure and equipment, and cost of economic measures)?

2. Are there specific sectors that have been, or would be, disproportionately affected by pandemics and epidemics (e.g., tourism, agriculture, manufacturing, etc.)?

5 Scrutiny

1 **Auditor General:** Are audit plans for the performance of epidemic/pandemic response or epidemic/pandemic arrangements in line with the International Standards of Supreme Audit Institutions 5520 (https://www.issai.org/wp-content/uploads/2019/08/issai-5520-e.pdf)?

2. **Auditor General:** Are audit reports available?

3. **Auditor General/Accountant General:** Are separate epidemic/pandemic expenditure report formats specified in financial rules?

4. **Auditor General/Accountant General:** Which separate financial and activity reports were produced from past epidemics/pandemics?

APPENDIX 4

Pandemic Risk Financing—The Enabling Environment Questionnaire for Insurance, Reinsurance, and Capital Market Solutions

1 Axis: Government Policy

Respondents are asked to assess the current and realistic enabling environment against the ideal enabling environment for each of the factors listed in the table below.

Current Environment	Realistic Enabling Environment	Ideal Enabling Environment
		Declared government policy on insurance, reinsurance, and capital market (IRCM) solutions *(Please describe the state of government policy supporting the development of IRCM solutions.)* *When responding to this question, please consider the various sectors affected by epidemics/pandemics as different sectors may have different protection policies. Please cover at least the following: sovereign protection, private sector protection in general, and low-income population protection.*
		Well-coordinated institutional arrangements for the application of IRCM solutions across relevant government ministries and agencies, including local government entities
		Well-complemented and coordinated roles of relevant government ministries and agencies on IRCM policy declaration and execution
		Customized regulation or other formal guidance of IRCM solutions for health, including epidemics/pandemics
		Tax incentives for the use of IRCM health solutions
		Tax incentives for providers of IRCM health solutions
		Tax-free premiums
		Premium subsidies
		Financial aid for commercially uninsurable risks
		Mandatory primary health-care cover for the population, either through direct government provision or the use of a social health insurance scheme
		Social health program sustainability regularly evaluated by an actuary or a similar expert
		Coverage for pandemics/epidemics under government provided health-care schemes and/or social health insurance
		Effective border control policies, including border health teams to screen for signs of communicable diseases (e.g., temperature checking machines, health declarations, etc.)

continued on next page

Table *continued*

Current Environment	Realistic Enabling Environment	Ideal Enabling Environment
		Strict policies governing animal–human interactions, including but not limited to wet markets and wildlife trade. Strong regulator in place that takes enforcement action and has a track record of prosecutions
		Policies and procedures in place for pandemic/epidemic emergency preparedness, including plans to limit contagion risks, plans for health-care infrastructure use and stockpiling
		Robust policies for public health, particularly communicable disease control
		Robust and well-coordinated public health messaging, resulting in a high level of population health literacy, particularly as it pertains to hygiene, sanitation, and the management of communicable disease

In completing the above table, please address the following items:

1. What is the government's policy and involvement regarding agricultural insurance? For example, does it offer
   a. insurance education? If yes, how is it offered (e.g., informational session, seminars, web/TV/radio communication, advisory services)?
   b. subsidies for health insurance? If yes, what types of subsidies are provided (e.g., premium, claim, financing loss assessment)?

2. Is there a law (or any other legislative document) on epidemic/pandemic coverage in insurance?

3. Does the government impose special requirements to insurance companies offering epidemic/pandemic insurance?

4. Insurance regulator: Is health insurance a separate type of insurance or a separate risk class or is it reported within property insurance?

5. What are the respective roles of central and provincial governments in the IRCM market regarding
   a. claims settlement?
   b. grievance redress?
   c. premium subsidy
      - nature (paid to commercial or government-owned insurer/s)?
      - scale (as % of premium)?
      - relative outlay (as % of annual government expense)?
   d. rate making and negotiation?
   e. making risk transfer products available?
   f. advertising and provision of additional information to support agricultural insurance?

4. What is the government's policy and degree of support regarding ex-post loss and coping mechanisms—e.g., the latest evidence (e.g., for the past 5 years) on compensation and relief to population affected by epidemics/pandemics?

2 Axis: Economic Conditions and Other Support Functions

Respondents are requested to assess the current and realistic enabling environment against the ideal enabling environment for each of the factors listed in the table below.

Current Environment	Realistic Enabling Environment	Ideal Enabling Environment
		Growing economy
		Manageable inflation
		Access to financial services
		Availability of affordable credit
		No foreign exchange and withholding tax (including permanent establishment) restrictions that could stymie (re)insurance transactions
		Well-developed extension services for health insurance
		Business continuity requirements for the insurance and capital market sectors
		Liquid and developed capital market, including a liquid secondary market
		Promotion of epidemic/pandemic risk reduction
		Comprehensive health risk data
		Professional financial services, including auditing
		Strong government technical epidemic/pandemic risk management capacity
		An established regulatory body for pharmaceuticals with expedited processes for approving emergency-use therapies
		High levels of clinical training, particularly in disease detection, to enable outbreaks to be effectively diagnosed and reported
		Containment facilities, either in hospitals or other suitable locations, specifically designed for infectious patients/disease outbreaks
		A high degree of multilateral cooperation with entities such as the World Health Organization to coordinate global pandemics and epidemics
		Hospital beds to population ratio is near the Organisation for Economic Co-operation and Development (OECD) average
		Doctor to population ratio is near OECD average
		Nurse to population ratio is near OECD average
		Sufficient critical equipment (CT scanners, MRI scanners, ventilators) to cope with existing demand and surge demand during a pandemic
		Nonhealth-care workers in frontline caregiving roles (e.g., social services, social workers, nursing home staff) trained in infection control and management
		Sufficient cold storage capacity across the country to cope with routine and surge demand (e.g., mass vaccination under a pandemic)
		Strong vaccination uptake rates for routine vaccinations (e.g., Measles, Mumps, and Rubella) and literacy among the population for vaccines

3 Axis: Product Availability and Affordability

Respondents are asked to assess the current and realistic enabling environment against the ideal enabling environment for each of the factors listed in the table below.

Current Environment	Realistic Enabling Environment	Ideal Enabling Environment
		Wide range of epidemic/pandemic insurance products available *(Please provide an overview of the existing epidemic/pandemic insurance and capital market solutions available.)*
		Consumer-centered development of products
		Affordability for the targeted consumers
		Convenient distribution channels
		Ease of premium payments, including premium financing
		Appropriate speed of claims payments
		No unreasonable exclusions
		Religious and cultural aspects reflected in product design
		Incentives for purchase of epidemic/pandemic protection products
		Mandatory insurance for epidemic/pandemic risks
		Capital market solutions such as epidemic/pandemic bonds available to transfer epidemic/pandemic risk *(Please describe any existing capital market products that are used by insurers or the government to transfer epidemic/pandemic risks. If those instruments are not yet available, please provide information on any initiative in this area.)*
		Business continuity insurance covers not excluding pandemics/epidemics
		Loss of income due to pandemics/epidemics such as inability to fulfill orders, shipping, etc. Mandatory slaughtering of infected animals, etc.
		Private health insurance products (including reimbursement plans and critical illness plans) that are commercially available, cover pandemic/epidemic risks

4 Axis: Credibility of Insurance and Capital Market Stakeholders

Respondents are asked to assess the current and realistic enabling environment against the ideal enabling environment for each of the factors listed in the table below.

Current Environment	Realistic Enabling Environment	Ideal Enabling Environment
		Reputable regulator overseeing modern insurance and capital market supervisory legislation *(Please provide an estimate of the level of compliance with the International Association of Insurance Supervisors and the International Organization of Securities Commissions principles and standards.)*
		Well-established and credible insurance and capital markets *(Please provide an overview of the insurance and capital markets with respect to the regulation and key market statistics.)*
		A solvent insurance market *(Please provide an overview of the solvency, risk management, and risk transfer requirements for insurers.)*
		Reliable rating agencies *(Please provide an overview of the rating agencies operating in the country, including whether they include internationally accepted agencies or local ones only.)*
		Active press reporting on insurance and capital markets
		Use of high-quality reinsurers and reinsurance brokers *(Please provide an overview of the legal requirements applicable to reinsurers and reinsurance brokers.)*
		Confidence in and an impeccable image of the insurance sector
		Confidence in and an impeccable image of the capital markets
		A fair pricing culture
		A fair claims payment culture
		Contracts capable of being enforced within a reliable judicial system
		Trained and ethical agents/brokers and reinsurance brokers
		Adequate availability of all insurance experts (actuaries, brokers, risk assessors, financial advisors, loss adjustors)
		Accessible and effective complaints and redress mechanisms in place for insurance and capital market transactions
		Transparent costs of available insurance, reinsurance, and capital market solutions
		Available products easily understood by targeted consumers
		No misleading advertisement
		Guarantee fund for insolvencies of insurers and broker–dealers

5 Axis: Social Protection Policy

Respondents are requested to assess the current and realistic enabling environment against the ideal enabling environment for each of the factors listed in the table below.

Current Environment	Realistic Enabling Environment	Ideal Enabling Environment
		An effective social protection strategy that includes insurance, reinsurance, and capital market (IRCM) solutions *(Please describe the current social protection strategy of the government. This should include all social insurance programs in place, the mode of execution, and some performance indicators.)*
		Provision of social protection only for risks that cannot be transferred to the private sector either as insurance, reinsurance, or capital market solutions
		An existing analysis of risks that can be transferred to the private sector to increase effectiveness and manage budgetary costs and implementation of its findings
		Cost equivalence for any similar protection products provided both by the government and the private sector
		No carving out risks necessary for IRCM solutions to be sustainable (In commercial insurance, there is often cross-subsidy between different risks covered. Carving out of the risks that support the cost of covering less commercially attractive risks would reduce the viability of insurance.)
		Targeted post-disaster public support for poor households only (Full public support for all affected households would bring into question the necessity of private insurance.)
		Government support for affected public due to pandemics or epidemics
		Available social assistance products not crowding out IRCM solutions *(Please describe the social assistance that is provided to agricultural and low-income populations, including conditional cash transfer programs for low-income populations, minimum crop support prices for seeds, fertilizer subsidies, etc.)*
		Initiatives under implementation to promote microinsurance and Takaful insurance
		Robust and well-regulated health insurance market complimenting public provision
		Shock-responsive social protection schemes duly in place to quickly cover poor people and those who fall into poverty/informality because of pandemic-induced economic downturn (schemes sufficiently financed, able to respond quickly, enabling database of beneficiaries and efficient payout mechanisms in place)

6 Axis: Competition to the Formal Sector from Informal and Unlicensed Providers

Respondents are asked to assess the current and realistic enabling environment against the ideal enabling environment for each of the factors listed in the table below.

Current Environment	Realistic Enabling Environment	Ideal Enabling Environment
		Enforced regulation of unlicensed insurance and capital market activity
		All health insurance providers are regulated by the insurance supervisor
		Viability of hospital and other health assistance plans evaluated by an actuary or similar expert
		Public awareness programs on the potential dangers of using unlicensed insurance providers
		Solvency requirements regarding unlicensed activity and the existence of a modern law to cover insolvencies of financial institutions, including insurers
		Regulation of cross-border insurance, reinsurance, and capital markets (IRCMs) to avoid regulatory arbitrage
		Technical pricing requirements
		No monopoly for the provision of IRCM solutions
		Equal taxation for equivalent products, independent of provider
		Licensed and regulated health providers

APPENDIX 5
Tools for Insurance, Reinsurance, and Capital Market Solutions in Disaster Risk Financing

1 Disaster Insurance

Definition

Insurance is a financial transaction by which the insured, a physical or legal person, transfers to an insurer its natural hazard risk in exchange of a payment (insurance premium). Providers of insurance are licensed and supervised insurance companies, captive insurers, and insurance pools, which are entities exclusively dedicated to the insurance activity. In some jurisdictions, nonlicensed insurance activity exists. Depending on how this activity is controlled, it could result in an inability to fulfill the claim payment after a disaster because of insufficient funds by the entity acting as an unlicensed insurer.

Main Usage

Major disaster risk entails a low frequency, high severity event (earthquake, flood, cyclone, tsunami, drought, etc.). Although exposure and vulnerability to these events can be reduced, significant residual risk may remain, so the transfer of the risk through insurance is appealing as a valid risk management strategy.

Advantages

- There is agreed well-defined benefit in case of a disaster event.
- Coverage can be purchased based on individual needs and risk appetite.
- Cost of coverage can be based on individual levels of risk.
- Insurers help with risk reduction and risk assessment.
- Disaster risk is managed by professionals.
- Costs for the protection, in the form of a fixed premium, are predictable.

Disadvantages

- Laypersons may find policies hard to understand because the policy wording contains legal language.
- Key risks or those risks that are seen as more important by consumers may be excluded.
- Policies often include a large combined monetary and percentage deductible on each and every loss, negating or diminishing the benefits of insurance.
- The claim ceiling may be insufficient to replace the insured property to the same pecuniary state enjoyed before the disaster event.
- Benefits are not clearly perceived as disaster events occur infrequently, so for many years the premium is paid but no tangible benefit is obtained.
- Claim settlement can be burdensome.

Preconditions

- Disaster risk awareness
- Enabling government policy with respect to the development of disaster insurance instruments, potentially including mandatory insurance cover and tax benefits on the premium payments
- Disaster risk product availability and affordability, including products for corporates, individual households, and low-income populations
- Credibility of the insurance sector, including with regard to the regulatory environment, the solvency and reputation of the insurance markets, and the availability of support of professionals such as actuaries, risk assessors, auditors, brokers, and loss adjusters
- Complementary social protection solutions, allowing low-income populations to enjoy social protection or support in the acquisition of insurance, while avoiding the crowding out of insurance solutions for people that can afford premiums
- No unlicensed competition. Insurance credibility and resilient insurance providers are important and can only be achieved if all insurance providers are licensed and supervised by the insurance regulator.

2 Disaster Reinsurance

Definition

Reinsurance is a financial transaction by which disaster risk and other insured risks assumed by an insurer in the original insurance policy are transferred (ceded) from the insurance company (cedent) to a reinsurance company (reinsurer) in exchange of a payment (reinsurance premium). Providers of reinsurance are professional reinsurers, which are entities exclusively dedicated to the activity of reinsurance. In most jurisdictions, however, insurance companies also are allowed to participate in reinsurance (Wehrhahn 2009). Reinsurers are able to effectively assume huge amounts of disaster risk because they diversify by accepting risks from around the world and maintain substantial amounts of capital to support the assumed risks.

Main Usage

Major disaster risk entails a low frequency, high severity event (earthquake, floods, cyclone, tsunami, drought, etc.). This risk is difficult to diversify at the primary insurer level. Hence, without additional risk transfer possibilities, insurers would not be in an economic position to accept this type of risk on their own. Insurers assuming disaster risk protect their balance sheet by entering into reinsurance agreements.

Advantages

- Geographic diversification of disaster risks when using global reinsurance
- Increased underwriting capacity of the insurance sector. By ceding part of the risk, insurers can technically accept higher volumes of disaster risk. This is particularly important for disaster insurance as the scale of exposure of an insurance company can be very large.
- Risk-based pricing of premiums as reinsurers have access to disaster risk

- Reduction in the volatility of insurance company financials and protection of ceding companies' balance sheets
- More predictability in profit and shareholder returns

Disadvantages

- Insurers transfer the underwriting risk but assume credit risk. Proper credit risk analysis of the reinsurer is critical.
- Premium pricing depends to some extent on global capacity available and could become prohibitive in the event of a quick succession of extreme events.
- Terms on the risks reinsured are dictated by the reinsurer and could be different from the original insurance policy. Thus, the original risk is only partially transferred, and insurers could be left with substantial risk in their books, even after reinsurance.
- Payment of claims could be a lengthy process, affecting the cash flows of the ceding company.
- Reinsurers may include "event limits" on their treaties, thus exposing ceding companies to the possibility of having to take back the un-reinsured portion of the claims.
- There is the possibility of exhausting the nonproportional excess of loss reinsurance protection after a natural hazard without reinstatement of the cover, thus leaving insurers unprotected against subsequent natural hazard events in the same country or region.

Preconditions

- Sound supervision of the insurance and reinsurance markets to guarantee effective products and timely payments of claims
- Availability of international reinsurers interested in acting in the given country.
- Availability of data and risk maps
- Minimum credit rating of the reinsurers by reputed rating agencies, such as AM Best, Fitch, and Standard & Poor's Global Ratings
- Appropriate supervision of reinsurance brokers acting in the region/country

3 Insurance-Linked Securities

Definition

Insurance-linked securities (ILS) are investment instruments that transform insurance risk into transparent and tradable capital market products. Investors take on insurance risk in exchange for a higher rate of return as compared with other securities free of that risk. The insurance risk materializes in the event that a predefined disaster event occurs, such as an earthquake or tropical cyclone of a certain intensity. ILS include categories of vehicles such as catastrophe bonds, longevity or mortality bonds, fully collateralized reinsurance agreements, and industry loss warranties.

Main Usage

Catastrophe or cat bonds and other types of ILS are usually issued in order to provide (re)insurance protection to insurers, reinsurers, governments, and corporations. ILS offer protection from a new pool of capital separate from traditional reinsurers, such as hedge funds and pension funds. Investor capital provides collateralized cover. The capital sits in a segregated collateral account with dedicated funds available to make payments should a qualifying event occur. This virtually eliminates the credit risk inherent in traditional (re)insurance (Swiss Re 2012).

Advantages

- Immediate access to funds once the trigger event has been confirmed
- Limited concern about counterparty credit in the event of an extremely large event as the claim amount is fully collateralized
- Predictable budgetary costs for the issuer of the bonds
- Tailor-made triggers to cover individual disaster risk contexts
- A diversified source of disaster risk financing, which is especially beneficial when there is shortage of retrocession capacity or hard pricing cycles in traditional reinsurance markets
- Multiyear pricing stability (terms of 3–5 years are typical for cat bonds)
- For investors, a source of investment that is uncorrelated to broader cycles in financial market performance, resulting in a higher degree of portfolio diversification

Disadvantages

- Complexity of the product. Securities are already complex, and including the triggers related to the underwriting risks adds complexity to the structure of the instrument.
- Costs may be relatively high if the volume of issuance is small. Transaction size varies from a minimum of around $100 million to $750 million or $1 billion (Swiss Re 2012).
- Basis risk exists as the triggers might not be totally correlated with the actual loss suffered.
- Investor appetite may differ from the desired triggers.
- Triggers may be difficult to assess.

Preconditions

- Sophisticated securities markets that are able to issue ILS
- Sophisticated investors looking to diversify their investments away from traditional forms of market risk
- Transparent product structures
- Transparent and robust disaster risk models
- Clearly defined triggers
- An enabling government policy including tax benefits for ILS investors, regulations that allow insurers and reinsurers to use ILS for capital relief, etc.
- Attractive returns for investors in the ILS markets
- Credibility of the securities sector, including with regard to the associated regulatory environment, credibility and reputation of sponsors, and the availability of professionals such as broker-dealers, rating agencies, actuaries, and auditors

4 Agricultural Indemnity Insurance

Definition

Agricultural indemnity insurance is a type of insurance that indemnifies the insured person against pure agricultural loss (i.e., crop or livestock). The loss is verified by a loss assessment process. The insured person could be the farmer or farmer group or an agricultural lender whose delinquency risks depend on the outcome of agricultural output.

The following forms of agriculture indemnity insurance products are presently popular:

- **Single-risk insurance:** Covers against one peril or risk (e.g., drought).
- **Combined (peril) insurance:** Covers a combination of several risks (two or more risks, mostly with hail as basic cover). In some countries, this type of insurance is also referred to as multirisk insurance.
- **Yield insurance:** Provides a yield guarantee, based on regional average yield or on individual historic yield, covering the main risks affecting yield (e.g., drought). In some countries (e.g., the United States), this type is also called combined or multiperil insurance.
- **Revenue insurance:** Combines yield and price risks coverage in a single insurance product. It can be product-specific or whole farm.
- **Farm-income protection insurance:** Covers losses to future income (e.g., future droughts) based on investments in long-term production, thereby reducing reliance on government assistance in times of need and building farmers' business resilience. It includes yields and price risks and also considers the costs of production. Usually, this type of insurance is not product-specific, instead covering whole-farm income.
- **Whole-farm insurance:** Consists of a combination of guarantees for different agricultural types of production on a farm. Depending on the coverage of the guarantees, it can be whole-farm yield, revenue, or income insurance (EU 2008).

Main Usage

Agricultural indemnity insurance provides coverage to farmers and agricultural lenders against the loss of crop or livestock. When purchased by agricultural lenders, it can also increase their risk appetite to lend to farmers who are not otherwise creditworthy and at better terms than uninsured risks.

Advantages

- **Low basis risk:** Indemnity insurance in comparison with index insurance has low basis risk (i.e., the claim amount nearly matches the actual loss suffered).
- **Less data requirement:** Indemnity insurance requires less data, as compared with index insurance, for the design and development products.
- **Reasonably transparent verification processes:** Losses are verified on the ground, usually in the presence of the insured farmers, although entailing some level of subjectivity.
- **Transparent settlements:** Payouts are based on the scale of damage and losses experienced, making settlements easy to understand and communicate.

Disadvantages

- **Onerous assessment processes:** As a claim is paid after assessing each loss, the loss assessment process can be onerous and costly. However, modern and affordable technology can reduce the time for loss assessment, keeping costs in check. Technology-based tools can also provide corroborative information to reinforce human loss assessment activities.

- **Costly assessments:** The onerous loss assessment process implies high assessment costs.
- **High risk of adverse selection and moral hazard:** Claim payments often rely on crop-cutting experiments, leaving room for manipulation. Adverse selection (i.e., the purchase of insurance by farmers that are more likely to experience claims) is more likely with indemnity than with index-based insurance. Moral hazard (i.e., farmers acting in a manner that leads to greater chances of the claim becoming payable) is also more likely with indemnity than with index-based insurance.

Preconditions

- **Historical loss, modeled loss, and exposure data:** This information is required for several aspects of the product design, product evaluation, and product pricing processes. Insurance can work for risks with low frequency and higher values, but the product needs to be designed such that the risks with higher frequency and lower values are not transferred to the insurer, but instead retained—and hopefully reduced—through risk reduction efforts of the farmer.
- **Subject specialists:** Worthy products are usually developed with assistance from subject specialists. It is therefore important to make sure that the product development team has access to the required types of expertise, either internally or externally (e.g., agronomists, modelers, underwriters, and actuaries).
- **Distribution channels:** Efficient distribution channels lead to low administrative costs for underwriting and claim settlement. It is possible that the insurer may have a captive distribution channel (e.g., its own sales force to distribute credit-linked insurance for agricultural risks). The insurance product's sales process often needs to be embedded into the main business activities of the insured persons.
- **Availability of reinsurance:** Crop and livestock claims depend upon weather and other natural hazards, which can affect the entire region of coverage in a relatively short time span. This can lead to large and often covariate losses for the insurer as well as higher demands on capital to demonstrate solvency. Reinsurers can accept such risks by covering geographically diverse regions over long periods of time within their already diversified lines of businesses. Therefore, reinsurance capacity becomes necessary for agricultural insurance, which inherently faces large and covariate risks.
- **Regulatory support:** Regulation can support agricultural index-based insurance in many ways: (i) by setting lighter solvency requirements due to the extremely short-tailed losses, if that is not the case under the existing solvency requirements; (ii) by providing a prompt redress mechanism on claim settlement; or (iii) by setting up data infrastructure and coordinating investment in data as a public good.

5 Agricultural Index and Parametric Insurance

Definition

Agricultural parametric insurance is a form of insurance that, ex ante, agrees to make a payment upon the occurrence of a trigger observation or event linked to the loss, rather than indemnifying the pure agricultural loss (i.e., crop or livestock). The trigger observation could be a decrease in average yield or prices in a predefined area—area yield index insurance or a trigger event based on weather-based indexes, satellite images, and so on.

In developing such products, it is necessary to understand the thin dividing line between parametric insurance and index-based insurance. A parametric insurance product typically works on a binary parameter with only two possible outcomes (e.g., death or contracting a critical illness). In such cases, either a full payout or no payout is made as only two outcomes are possible. In contrast, index-based insurance is offered on parameters that most likely have multiple outcomes (wind velocity, precipitation levels, etc.) and can result in a graded scale of payouts. In such cases, claims are often linked to the trigger in a gradual manner (e.g., the farther above the observation from the trigger, the higher the claim payout) until a pre-agreed ceiling is reached.

The insured person could be the farmer or farmer group or lender whose delinquency risks depend on the outcome of agricultural output.

The following forms of agriculture indemnity insurance products are presently popular:

- **Area yield index insurance:** Indemnities are computed from the decrease in the average yield over an area without ascertaining crop output of individual farmers.
- **Area revenue index insurance:** Indemnities are computed from the decrease in the production of the average yields and prices in an area (EU 2008), without ascertaining crop output and prices of individual farmers.
- **Indirect index insurance:** Indemnities are based on indexes of yields or vegetation that are computed from weather-based indexes, satellite images, and others (EU 2008).

Main Usage

Agricultural parametric insurance provides security to farmers and agricultural lenders by eliminating the element of subjectivity in loss verification and reducing the time to settle claims. When purchased by agricultural lenders, it can also increase their appetite to lend to farmers who are not otherwise creditworthy and to lend on better terms for farmers.

Advantages

- **Low moral hazard:** Since the amount of payment is unaffected by the loss experienced, insured farmers (both crop and livestock) have an incentive to act in a manner that minimizes their losses, reducing issues of moral hazard.
- **Low adverse selection problem:** Similarly, parametric insurance reduces the risk of adverse selection as payouts are based on widely available information, rather than on individual loss experience and related risk about which insurance companies may not have full information.
- **Easier loss assessment:** Since the claim payment is dependent on a trigger, efforts in assessing losses (e.g., deploying loss assessors on-site and seeking inputs) are substantially minimized.
- **Prompt claim settlement:** As actual loss assessment is not needed, claim settlement can be prompt after reading off the index.

Disadvantages

- **Basis risk:** Index-based insurance, unlike indemnity insurance, carries basis risk. This is the risk that the index measurements that trigger the insurance payout will not match actual loss experienced. The payout could be less or more than the experienced loss. Basis risk can reduce customer satisfaction and affect continuity of an insurance program.
- **Model risk:** If robust modeling tools and techniques are not used, the loss frequency results may be incorrect, leading to inappropriate pricing and, in turn, directly affecting client satisfaction and the uptake of insurance.
- **Substantial data requirements:** Rate making and trigger definition require a large amount of weather and crop yield data. Insufficient data can lead to incorrect decisions on rate making and product design.
- **Complexity:** Farmers may face difficulties in comprehending the linkage between triggers and losses and the overall benefits of index-based insurance.
- **High product development costs:** Subject experts and data infrastructure are required for the design of parametric insurance, increasing product development cost.

Preconditions

- **Historical and modeled weather data:** This information is required for several stages of product design, evaluation, and pricing. If such information is not available, designing a robust product will not be feasible.
- **Subject experts:** Valuable products are usually designed with assistance from subject specialists. It is important to make sure that the product development team is multiskilled (e.g., in crop agronomy and statistical modeling) and has the necessary experience and expertise to develop the required products.
- **Historical and modeled loss data:** Especially for area yield index insurance, historical and modeled loss data are essential in pricing the product and determining the trigger.
- **Real-time hazard data:** Real-time hazard data are required to provide prompt payouts and maintain customer satisfaction.
- **Product design capabilities:** High-quality product design capabilities must be available to the insurer, either internally (in the long run) or externally (in the short run).
- **Regulatory and supervisory support:** Regulation can support agricultural index-based insurance in many ways: (i) by setting lighter solvency requirements due to the extremely short-tailed losses, if it is not the case in the existing regulations; (ii) by recognizing index insurance, which could otherwise be argued as a "derivative" product; (iii) by setting up data infrastructure and coordinating investment in data as a public good; or (iv) by setting up a supervisory mechanism that emphasizes education of farmers on parametric products.
- **Distribution channels:** Proper distribution channels are required to help ensure low administrative costs for underwriting and claim settlement.
- **Availability of reinsurance:** Index insurance is normally used to transfer covariant risks that can affect a whole country or region at the same time, necessitating access of insurers to sufficient reinsurance capacity.
- **Weather infrastructure:** A sufficient network of tamper-proof weather stations and satellite imaging infrastructure are required to capture data regularly and accurately.
- **Animal mortality rates:** In case of mortality index-based livestock insurance, historical animal mortality rates (including exposure and death events) by species, time, and geography are necessary.

6 Sovereign Parametric Insurance

Definition

Like any parametric insurance, sovereign parametric insurance, ex ante, agrees to make a payment upon the occurrence of a trigger observation or an event linked to the loss, rather than indemnifying the pure loss. It may be purchased by the government of a sovereign state and works on the usual insurance principles of premium payment to cover risks. The trigger observations can be specified intensities of natural hazards in a specified location (e.g., rainfall level, wind speed, seismic shocks as measured on a Richter scale) as measured by an independent agency. Claim payouts could be linear (i.e., gradually increasing claims paid as the actual observation moves beyond the parametric trigger) or categorical (i.e., payment of a fixed sum on the breaching of the defined parametric trigger).

Main Usage

Parametric insurance may be used to provide security to a country's fiscal position while reducing the element of subjectivity in loss verification and time to settle claims. It also reduces the post-disaster fiscal stress on the insured country, hence smoothing government spending. Parametric cover is suitable for low-frequency, high-severity events.

Advantages

- **Fiscal support:** Sovereign insurance reduces potential post-disaster budget reallocations, which in turn may derail achievement of a government's development goals.
- **Easier loss assessment:** Since the claim payment is dependent on a trigger, efforts in assessing losses are substantially minimized and objectivity is increased.
- **Prompt claim settlement:** As actual loss assessment is not needed, claim settlement can be very prompt, occurring within just 2–3 weeks following an event.
- **Low operating cost:** Operating costs are low relative to traditional insurance products due to the simplicity of sales and loss adjustment, the lack of need to classify policyholders according to their risk exposure, and the lack of asymmetric information (Agroinsurance 2008).
- **Low moral hazard:** As the amount for payouts is unaffected by the loss experienced, governments have an incentive to act in a manner that minimizes losses, reducing issues of moral hazard.

Disadvantages

- **Basis risk:** Index-based insurance, unlike indemnity insurance, carries basis risk. This is the risk that the index measurements that trigger the insurance payout will not match actual loss experienced. The payout could be less or more than the experienced loss.
- **Model risk:** If robust modeling tools and techniques are not used, the frequency results can be incorrect, leading to inappropriate pricing and, in turn, directly affecting client satisfaction and the uptake of insurance.
- **High start-up costs:** Despite low operating cost, index insurance can have high start-up cost, especially in the absence of appropriate weather data and skilled

meteorological expertise. The readiness of a country to buy the parametric insurance cover depends in part on its existing infrastructure, such as with regard to an asset inventory, meteorological data, hazard maps, exposure data, vulnerability analyses, historical disaster data, and disaster risk models.

- **Data requirements:** Rate making and trigger definition require a large amount of data, such as on exposed assets (including public assets), past and modeled hazard events, and weather. The absence of data can lead to incorrect decisions on rate making and product design.

Preconditions

- **Understanding of disaster risk:** Parametric cover is best applicable to very low-frequency, high-severity events.
- **Data infrastructure:** Weather and seismology-related information is required for several stages of product design, evaluation, pricing, and implementation. Information should be capable of independent verification using different tools. For example, satellite images can complement a primary weather station's information regarding precipitation. If this type of information is not available, it may not be possible to design an appropriate product.
- **Subject experts:** Valuable products are usually designed with assistance from subject specialists. It is important to make sure that the product development team is multiskilled and has the required experience and expertise. Often, there is a need to involve reinsurance companies interested in underwriting the cover to provide domain expertise.
- **Historical and modeled loss data:** Historical and modeled loss data are essential in pricing the product as well as in defining the trigger. Insufficient or inappropriate data could give rise to gaps in coverage or other serious product-related issues.
- **Real-time hazard data:** In the absence of real-time data, it is difficult to gauge the amount of claim payment in a timely manner.
- **Frequency and accuracy of recording data:** Weather stations and satellite imaging infrastructure need to capture data regularly and accurately and be highly resistant to any form of tampering. This type of infrastructure is critical to assessing whether a particular area has breached the trigger.

7 Insurance Pool

Definition

An insurance pool is a multiple-member risk-sharing arrangement where organizations (often primary underwriters) pool their funds together to finance an exposure, liability, risk, or some combination of the three. Pools can have layers of coverage, such as insurance, excess insurance, and different deductibles for different members.

Main Usage

An insurance pool can create capacity at multiple dimensions: supply of insurance for business lines that face high risks from unfavorable outcomes, underwriting of large risks by pool members, technical capacity for development of complex insurance products, advice and information gathering for loss assessment, stability of underwriting results, and reduction of the impact of single, large risks.

Advantages

Designing an insurance pool should consider the following factor (ADB 2019d):

- **Product design:** Undertaking product design and providing support on an ongoing basis are more efficient when a centralized pool gathers information.
- **Information gathering:** Being a repository of losses, the pool is able to undertake more in-depth analysis.
- **Leverage:** A pool can leverage its collective buying power as a block to negotiate premium and deductibles to the comparative advantage of its members.
- **Customization:** The scale of provision of member services, including risk control, claims management, and training, is sufficient to support customization.
- **Innovation:** A pool is better able to support the insurance industry's development of innovative products and offer unique forms of coverage, particularly with regard to efficient and cheap technology for indemnity and area yield index products.
- **Flexibility:** A pool is better able to respond to the needs of individual insurers through variable deductibles, self-insured retention levels, and special coverage.
- **Subsidy policy:** A pool can provide data that could be useful to guide policy on premium subsidies, which in principle should be restricted to the cost of underwriting systemic risks.
- **Credibility:** By involving many key public sector stakeholders (e.g., the regulator and other government departments), pool members can demonstrate higher credibility to supply insurance.
- **Pricing stability:** Pools can involve a layer of capital to cover the first layer of losses, reducing use of reinsurance and resulting in greater price stability.
- **Reinsurance:** Economies of scale facilitate the purchase of reinsurance at a more competitive price.

Disadvantages

- **Lower diversification:** Disaster and/or agriculture insurance pools face high covariate risk from lower diversification, which can be detrimental to their solvency.
- **Cost:** The management of an insurance pool involves direct costs (e.g., secretariat overhead, salary, system cost) and indirect costs (e.g., time of regulators and other government officials).
- **Speed of decision-making:** As a pool involves policy decisions that can simultaneously affect all members, decisions are based on deliberations among pool members. Individual underwriters, on the other hand, can make prompt business decisions.

Preconditions

- **Reinsurance:** An agriculture or disaster insurance pool will have high covariate risks. It is imperative to have proper reinsurance arrangements to maintain the solvency of the pool.
- **Regulatory framework:** Insurance pools involve many stakeholders and underwrite large, collective risks. In order to prevent conflict, it is necessary to have rules or regulations in place to demarcate the rights and duties of all the stakeholders.

- **Subject experts:** Managing a pool's risks and information keeping requires subject specialists. Often, it requires involving subject specialists who have a strong understanding of the specific risks being pooled as well as an in-depth understanding of the pool's reinsurance arrangements.
- **Medium- and long-term strategies:** As insurance pools are often created to address a market need in the medium (3–5 years) and long term (5–10 years), a well-planned strategy is necessary to envisage future functioning. For example, a strategy may consider winding up a pool after certain performance parameters have been achieved.
- **Information systems:** Adequate information technology systems are needed to record data, settle distribution costs and claims, and demonstrate solvency.

Glossary

Agricultural indemnity insurance

A type of insurance that indemnifies the insured person against pure agricultural loss (i.e., crop or livestock). The loss is determined on the basis of a traditional loss adjustment process. The insured person could be the farmer or farmer group or lender whose delinquency risks depend on the outcome of agricultural output.

Agricultural parametric insurance

A type of insurance that agrees to make a payment upon the occurrence of a triggering event, rather than indemnifying the pure agricultural loss (i.e., crop or livestock). The trigger observation could be the decrease in average yield or prices in an area (i.e., area yield index insurance) or a trigger event read off weather-based indexes, satellite images, and so on. The insured person could be the farmer or farmer group or lender whose delinquency risks depend on the outcome of agricultural output.

Average annual loss

The expected value of the modeled loss distribution, or the loss one would expect to see in a year on average. A key risk model output is a fully probabilistic loss distribution, which is typically expressed as an exceedance probability curve. The mean of this distribution is the average annual loss (AAL) or the expected loss per year, averaged over many years. AAL is a loss statistic that is widely used and has a diverse range of applications in disaster risk management (Air Worldwide 2013).

Basis risk

The risk, with index insurance, that the index measurements that trigger the insurance payout will not match actual loss experienced. The payout could be less or more than the experienced loss.

Captive insurance

The provision of insurance or reinsurance by a subsidiary company for its parent company.

Catastrophe bond

A high-yielding, insurance-linked security providing for payment of interest and/or principal to be suspended or cancelled in the event of a specified disaster, such as an earthquake of a certain magnitude or above within a predefined geographical area (World Bank 2012b).

Claim provisions

Represent the estimated liability of an insurance company arising from events that have occurred on or before the valuation date. The provisions should cover the future payment of incurred claims that have not been settled, whether such claims have been reported or not. Claim provisions are a liability on the balance sheet because they are the anticipated amounts that will have to be paid to policyholders as the incurred claims are gradually settled and paid out. The monetary amount of the claim provision can be calculated subjectively (using the judgment of claim assessors or of insurance company claim specialists) or statistically (by evaluating past experience and projecting loss development into the future).

Contingent disaster financing

A pre-agreed loan or grant that disburses after pre-agreed conditions have been met. In terms of disaster risk financing, the contingent trigger is often the declaration of a state of emergency.

Disaster

A sudden, calamitous event that seriously disrupts the functioning of a community or society, causing widespread human, material, economic, or environmental losses that exceed the community's or society's ability to cope using its own resources. Disasters result from a combination of hazards, vulnerability, and inability to reduce the potential negative consequences of risk (ADB 2004).

Disaster insurance

The insurance to protect businesses and residences against natural hazards such as earthquakes, floods, and hurricanes. It can also apply to human-made disasters such as terrorism events.

Disaster risk

The probability of a disaster of a specific magnitude occurring.

Disaster risk (or catastrophe) model

A model based on a large set of simulated scenarios for the peril under consideration, which has been developed to capture the full range of potential impacts from that peril. Each simulated scenario is associated with an annual rate of occurrence, enabling the model to quantify the probability with which any given level of impact can be expected to occur (ADB 2018).

Exceedance probability (or annual rate of exceedance)

The probability that the maximum loss within an annual period from a single event will exceed a range of loss thresholds (ADB 2018).

Exposure

The presence of assets such as buildings and infrastructure that, when impacted by an event, can generate a financial loss for the parties responsible.

Hazard

A process, phenomenon, substance, human activity or condition that may cause loss of life, injury or other health impacts, property damage, loss of livelihoods and services, social and economic disruption, or environmental damage (UNISDR 2017b).

Indemnity

An insurance structure whose payout is determined by the actual losses suffered by the insured.

Insurance

A risk transfer mechanism that ensures full or partial financial compensation for the loss or damage caused by event(s) beyond the control of the insured party.

Insurance-linked securities

Specialized financial instruments that are sold to investors, including catastrophe bonds and other forms of risk-linked securitization.

Insurance pool

A multiple-member risk-sharing arrangement where organizations (often primary underwriters) pool their funds together to finance an exposure, liability, risk, or some combination of the three. Pools can have layers of coverage, such as insurance, excess insurance, and different deductibles for different members.

Long-tail and short-tail insurance liability

A long-tail insurance liability represents a liability for a claim that will have a long settlement period. These types of claims, typically in liability and related lines, are likely to result in high-incurred but not reported claim amounts because they frequently take a long period before such claims are reported. Even after being reported, settlement may take significant time, because litigation is often required in order to finally determine the amount that should be paid by the insurer. By comparison, a short-tail insurance liability will be settled quickly after its occurrence. Typical short-tail claims involve lines such as theft and fire. Estimating the required claim provisions for an insurance business with long-tailed liabilities is a difficult task, but the estimate can be very significant.

Loss ratio

The total claim costs against the total premiums earned for that coverage. It is used by insurers to determine the adequacy of the premium.

Microinsurance

Insurance that is designed to be accessed by low-income populations. It can be provided by a variety of different entities but is run in accordance with generally accepted insurance practices (which should include the International Association of Insurance Supervisors Insurance Core Principles). Importantly, this means that the risk insured under a microinsurance policy is managed based on insurance principles and funded by premiums (IAIS 2007).

Parametric insurance

A type of insurance trigger mechanism for which insurance payouts are determined based on physical hazard measurements (e.g., wind speed or earthquake magnitude) rather than actual losses suffered by the insured (ADB 2018).

Probable maximum loss

The probability that the maximum loss from a single event within an annual period will exceed a range of loss thresholds (ADB 2018).

Regulation

Various legal instruments with binding power. These instruments include legislation, which is usually issued by the parliament, and subordinate legislation issued by the regulator or supervisor.

Reinsurance

The insurance that insurance companies purchase to ensure that their retained risks do not exceed their available capital resources, to reduce volatility in underwriting results, and for other reasons.

Return period

The time frame over which a particular loss threshold can be expected to be exceeded at least once.

Risk-based capital

An amount of capital based on an assessment of risks that a company should hold to protect customers against adverse developments (Nicoletti 2016). As an insurer's risk level increases, its required capital level should also increase by a sufficient amount to ensure that the overall net risk of the insurer remains the same.

Risk layering

The process of separating risk into tiers depending on the probability of occurrence. Risk layering allows for establishing a more efficient strategy to finance and manage risks.

Risk transfer

The transfer of risk from one party to another through for example, an insurance policy (ADB 2018).

Social insurance

Government schemes in which social contributions are paid by employees or others, or by employers on behalf of their employees, to secure entitlement to social insurance benefits, in the current or subsequent periods, for the employees or other contributors, their dependents, or survivors (OECD 2008).

Social protection

The set of public actions designed to address vulnerability or chronic poverty. These interventions are most often carried out by the state but can also involve other actors, such as commercial companies, charitable organizations, and self-help groups.

Supervision

The effort to ensure compliance with regulation. A supervisory agency is a statutory body that enforces compliance of regulated entities with an existing regulation, such as with the help of sanctions provided for in the supervisory statute. Today, much financial supervision is of a type referred to as risk-based. This means that, rather than attempting to enforce strict compliance with a defined set of rules that are incorporated into the law, the supervisor's task is to monitor risk levels in supervised institutions and, making use of various types of preventive and corrective measures that are set out in the law (e.g., the power to require an institution to slow down its rate of growth or to increase the size of its capital base), to cause risk levels to be reduced when they become excessive.

References

Agroinsurance. 2008. Weather Index Insurance for Agriculture and Rural Area in Lower-Income Countries. 16 January. https://agroinsurance.com/en/2968/.

Air Worldwide. 2013. *Aircurrents: Modeling Fundamentals: What is Average Annual Loss*. 25 March. https://www.air-worldwide.com/SiteAssets/Publications/AIR-Currents/2013/Attachments/Modeling-Fundamentals--What-Is-AAL-.

Asian Development Bank (ADB). 2004. *Disaster and Emergency Assistance Policy*.

——. 2014. *Operational Plan for Integrated Disaster Risk Management, 2014–2020*.

——. 2018. *Philippine City Disaster Insurance Pool: Pool Rationale and Design*.

——. 2019a. *The Enabling Environment for Disaster Risk Financing in Fiji: Country Diagnostics Assessment*.

——. 2019b. *The Enabling Environment for Disaster Risk Financing in Pakistan: Country Diagnostics Assessment*.

——. 2019c. *The Enabling Environment for Disaster Risk Financing in Sri Lanka: Country Diagnostics Assessment*.

——. 2019d. *The Enabling Environment for Disaster Risk Financing in Nepal: Country Diagnostics Assessment*.

——. 2020. *Assessing the Enabling Environment for Disaster Risk Financing: A Country Diagnostics Tool Kit*.

ADB and World Bank. 2017. *Assessing Financial Protection Against Disasters: A Guidance Note on Conducting a Disaster Risk Finance Diagnostic*.

Chandwani, S. 2020. Data Protection and Privacy in the Insurance Industry. *Entrepreneur India*. 5 March. https://www.entrepreneur.com/article/347212.

European Union (EU). 2008. *Agriculture Insurance Schemes*. Joint Research Center and Institute for the Protection and Security of the Citizen.

Feldblum, S. 2011. Rating Agencies. *Casualty Actuarial Society*. 3 October.

Financial Accounting Standards Board. 2008. *Insurance–Risk Transfer*. Project Updates. 20 June.

Global Facility for Disaster Reduction and Recovery (GFDRR). Disaster Risk Finance. https://www.gfdrr.org/en/disaster-risk-finance.

——. 2014. *Understanding Risk in an Evolving World: Emerging Best Practices in Disaster Risk Assessment*. https://www.gfdrr.org/sites/default/files/publication/Understanding_Risk-Web_Version-rev_1.8.0.pdf.

Hofman, D. 2007. Time to Master Disaster. *Finance and Development*. 44 (1). International Monetary Fund. https://www.imf.org/external/pubs/ft/fandd/2007/03/hofman.htm.

International Association of Insurance Supervisors (IAIS). 2007. *Issues in Regulation and Supervision of Microinsurance*.

Leavitt Group. 2023. Prepare for Disaster with Business Interruption Insurance. 20 January. https://news.leavitt.com/business-insurance/business-interruption-insurance/.

Marsh & McLennan Companies. 2018. *Parametric Insurance: A Tool to Increase Climate Resilience*. https://www.mmc.com/insights/publications/2018/dec/parametric-insurance-tool-to-increase-climate-resilience.html.

McConaghy, P. 2017. Disaster Risk Insurance to Promote Resilience. *CGAP Blog Series: Financial Services in Humanitarian Crises*. 6 June. https://www.cgap.org/blog/disaster-risk-insurance-promote-resilience.

Merkin, R. and J. Steele. 2013. *Insurance and the Law of Obligations*. Oxford University Press.

Monti, A. 2011. *Policy Framework for the Improvement of Financial Management Strategies to Cope with Large-Scale Catastrophe in Chile*. Paper prepared for the High-Level Roundtable on the Financial Management of Earthquakes. Paris. 23–24 June.

Nicoletti, B. 2016. *Digital Insurance: Business Innovation in the Post-Crisis Era*. Palgrave Macmillan.

Organisation for Economic Co-operation and Development (OECD). 2008. *OECD Glossary of Statistical Terms*. https://www.oecd.org/en/publications/oecd-glossary-of-statistical-terms_9789264055087-en.html.

——. 2012. *Disaster Risk Assessment and Risk Financing: A G20/OECD Methodological Framework*. OECD Publishing. https://doi.org/10.1787/8f48d476-en.

——. 2013. *Disaster Risk Financing in APEC Economies: Practices and Challenges*. Report prepared for the meeting of APEC Finance Ministries. Indonesia. 19–20 September.

——. 2018. *Developing the Elements of a Disaster Risk Financing Strategy:* Conference Outcomes. Bangkok. 8–9 May. http://www.oecd.org/pensions/insurance/Developing-elements-of-disaster-risk-financing-strategy-May-2018-conference-outcomes.pdf.

Patwardhan, A. 2018. Chapter 4 – Financial Inclusion in the Digital Age. *In D. L. K. Chuen and R. Deng, eds. Handbook of Blockchain, Digital Finance, and Inclusion*. Volume 1. Academic Press. pp. 57–89. https://doi.org/10.1016/B978-0-12-810441-5.00004-X.

Rawle, K. O. 2013. *Financing Natural Catastrophe Exposure: Issues and Options for Improving Risk Transfer Markets. Congressional Research Service*. https://fas.org/sgp/crs/misc/R43182.pdf.

Schiffer, L. 2004. Insurer Insolvency and Reinsurance. Expert Commentary. *International Risk Management Institute, Inc.* 1 July. https://www.irmi.com/articles/expert-commentary/insurer-insolvency-and-reinsurance.

Skipper, H. D. Jr., and R. W. Klein. 2000. Insurance Regulation in the Public Interest: The Path Towards Solvent, Competitive Markets. *The Geneva Papers on Risk and Insurance*. 25 (4). pp. 482–504. https://link.springer.com/content/pdf/10.1111/1468-0440.00078.pdf.

Starita, M. G. and I. Malafronte. 2014. *Capital Requirements, Disclosure, and Supervision in the European Insurance Industry: New Challenges Towards Solvency II*. Palgrave Macmillan.

Swiss Re. 2012. *What Are Insurance Linked Securities (ILS), and Why Should They be Considered?* Presentation to the CANE Fall Meeting. September. https://www.casact.org/sites/default/files/presentation/affiliates_cane_0912_cat-bond.pdf.

Tennyson, S. 2010. Incentive Effects of Community Rating in Insurance Markets: Evidence from Massachusetts Automobile Insurance. *The Geneva Risk and Insurance Review*. 35(1). pp. 19–46. http://dx.doi.org/10.1057/grir.2010.2.

United Nations Office for Disaster Risk Reduction (UNISDR). 2015. *Global Assessment Report on Disaster Reduction 2015*. https://www.preventionweb.net/english/hyogo/gar/2015/en/home/.

——. 2017a. *National Disaster Risk Assessment: Governance System, Methodologies, and Use of Results*. https://www.unisdr.org/files/52828_nationaldisasterriskassessmentpart1.pdf.

——. 2017b. *UNISDR Terminology on Disaster Risk Reduction*.

Vathana, S., O. Oum, P. Kan, and C. Chervier. 2013. Impact of Disasters and Role of Social Protection in Disaster Risk Management in Cambodia. *ERIA Discussion Paper Series*. No. 10. Economic Research Institute for ASEAN and East Asia. https://www.eria.org/ERIA-DP-2013-10.pdf.

Wehrhahn, R. F. 2009. *Introduction to Reinsurance*. World Bank.

——. 2010. Insurance Underutilization in Emerging Economies: Causes and Barriers. In C. Kempler, M. Flamée, C. Yang, and P. Windels, eds. Global Perspectives on Insurance Today. Palgrave Macmillan.

White, D. W. 1998. Bad Faith Litigation in Massachusetts: The Plaintiff's Perspective. *Breakstone, White & Gluck*. October. https://www.bwglaw.com/bad-faith-litigation-in-massachusetts-the-plaintiff-s-perspectiv.html.

Willis Towers Watsons. 2017. What is Alternative Risk Transfer? https://www.willistowerswatson.com/en-US/insights/2017/08/what-is-alternative-risk-transfer.

Wolters Kluwer. 2018. *The Insurance Compliance Manager's Guide to Modernizing Complaints' Management*. http://www.wolterskluwerfs.com/insurance-compliance/white-paper/modernizing-complaints-management.aspx.

Workman, R. 2015. *Fair Treatment for the Insured: ICP 19 Conduct of Business*. A presentation of the International Association of Insurance Supervisors. Chile. 2 December. https://www.assalweb.org/assal_nueva/documentos/upload/5.2_R.Workman.pdf.

World Bank. 2012a. *Advancing Disaster Risk Financing and Insurance in ASEAN Member States: Framework and Options for Implementation*.

——. 2012b. *FONDEN: Mexico's Disaster Fund – A Review*.

——. 2015. Agricultural Risk Management in the Face of Climate Change. *Agriculture Global Practice Discussion Paper*. No. 9.

www.ingramcontent.com/pod-product-compliance
Ingram Content Group UK Ltd.
Pitfield, Milton Keynes, MK11 3LW, UK
UKHW062014041026
15591UKWH00017B/1331

9 789292 772482